Confessions of a Corporate Sycophant***

"A Humorous Look at a Career in Public Relations."

***The word "sycophant" is defined in the first chapter...

By
JOHN LANDSBERG

Copyright © 2013 John Landsberg
All rights reserved.
ISBN: 1480147079
ISBN 13: 9781480147072

Dedication

First, I would like to thank my wife of four decades, Donnamarie, for pestering me over the years with her ongoing encouragement, "You ought to write a book about this stuff. People won't believe it."

Well, honey, as usual, I listened to your wise advice, and here's the darn book.

My son, Todd, and daughter, Jenny, also followed their mother's lead in nagging me to pen the stories I have shared with them for years about my career in PR. Maybe that's why Todd is an audiologist today and the Jenny is an architect.

My family knows. I have the attention span of a gnat and that discipline is not my strong suit. Sitting down and writing a book was a real challenge. The nagging worked.

I would also like to thank all my co-workers during my career. The many stories I relate in this book gave us all a good laugh (or tears) for years

I would also like to thank my mother, St. Donna of Landsberg, for always being a positive

influence in my life. She supported me even when I really didn't deserve it.

All in all, being in public relations has given me a wonderful career and put me in the center of corporate life, where I could frequently witness first-hand Toto pulling the curtain back on the Wizard of Oz. And I tried to explain it all.

Let me conclude my dedication on that Oz analogy…

Foreword

All things considered, there are very few things that get me as excited as dealing with the media. Whether it's being proactive and pitching a story to them, or reactive by trying to put a happy face on a potential crisis, it is really something I relish. I still get excited when a positive article that I helped to place appears in the news.

Sometimes, though, working for companies that want to portray themselves as warm, caring, customer- and quality-focused "families" can be quite a task. In reality the majority of them are just the opposite.

If our real families acted in the same manner, nobody would ever get married. That's where the challenge comes in for communicators. Kind of the lipstick on a pig theory…

And that is the overriding focus of this book: that there is so much lying, BS and crapola today in business that it often undermines the entire corporate world. Executives lie to their employees; employees lie back to them. Pretty soon the whole business process is undermined and businesses and their employees suffer. It turns into a classic lose-lose proposition.

Let me speak briefly about my chosen profession as a PR professional.

Let's face it, calling yourself a PR guy is not necessarily up there with "surgeon" or "architect."

I came to that realization years ago while watching the TV show "Dynasty." I rarely actually watched the show, but it featured the distinguished actor John Forsythe playing corporate oil tycoon "Blake Carrington," who was always dealing with some major corporate issue.

In the episode I watched Carrington's business was on the brink of collapse. Everything was falling apart and he was about to go down for the count.

In the midst of this disaster Carrington's dingy, spoiled daughter showed up and says something like "Daddy, your business is in the crapper and I want to help you out."

At that point the dashing Carrington replied with something like, "Oh, honey, you have no talents whatsoever and have the brains of a minnow. You are really a walking Vegematic and have nothing to offer."

"But, daddy, I want to help you," says Vegematic cutely.

At that point Carrington gave his daughter a paternalistic look and said, "Okay, dear, you can work in the Public Relations Department."

At that moment I realized in the eyes of Hollywood my position might not have been the most respected job in the corporate world. In fact, it wasn't respected at all.

But I also realized I had already been in PR for about 10 years. My corporate life was pretty much set in stone. Hey, court jesters have to make a living, too…

My background in communications has brought me into contact with all levels of employees on a daily basis. Unfortunately, in today's work environment the gap between the executive staffers of a company and the actual worker bees has grown dramatically.

Executives today think their employees are stupid, lazy malcontents. Employees think the executives have their heads up their butts and feel they are just greedy pigs who will screw them on a moment's notice.

In all honesty, the truth is somewhere in between.

In reality, most organizations look at customers as faceless blobs they reluctantly have to deal with. "Things certainly would run smoother around here if we didn't have to deal with the damn customer" could be a real slogan of most companies today, but you won't see it on one of their motivational posters in the hall.

Their printed slogans are just the opposite: "Everything we do is to serve the customer," or "The customer is always right," or "We are a customer-focused company." Employees look at those hokey posters and mumble, "Yeah, right!"

To further illustrate this point, I have always found it ironic that many of the cheapest, lowest-status, highest-stress jobs in an organization are the ones where employees have to deal with actual customers. Sales clerks, telephone operators, and telemarketers are paid like recent immigrants and treated with the same status.

Basically, the corporate rule of thumb is that as you rise in an organization, you are rewarded by getting to move farther away from the customer. Heck, the great thing in corporate America today is that when you reach the upper, upper levels, then you rarely have to deal with customers—or even your own employees. This is true executive nirvana: Customers *and* employees are nameless, faceless blobs.

Most of my corporate experience involved working with all kinds of media people—newspaper, TV and radio folks on various media beats. I have also been involved with the sports media—known in journalistic circles as "Clown Town"—which used to be fun.

Over time, however, sportswriters have begun to deal more with high-finance issues and controversies than even their "real" journalistic counterparts in the business and editorial sections.

I hope this book provides some insights into the corporate world that I have garnered from my 25-plus years in the field. Much of it will look at issues from a communications/media point of view, but I hope everyone in the corporate world can relate to many of these stories.

It should be noted that many of the corporate types I dealt with were female, but for the sake of simplicity I refer to them as "he" throughout this book.

In all honesty, I have had the great fortune to work with some wonderful people at some super companies. I have also worked with my fair share of dipsticks and incompetents at some really crappy companies. Over time it balances out.

The one common thread that I brought to the table was generating positive publicity for all my companies, no matter how stupidly they behaved. That was my goal as a corporate sycophant and I did it pretty well.

Public Relations is a 24/7 job. You are always on-call. What may have started out as a wonderful day can turn into crap with a single phone call from a reporter or executive. The cover of this book summarizes that thought quite well.

Without further ado, let's get into it. And, to show what a nice guy I am, I will let you know what a "sycophant" is in the first chapter. I don't believe in keeping people in suspense.

Book Chapters

Chapter 1:	"Confessions Of A Corporate Sycophant"....... 1
Chapter 2:	Trying To Manage Those Media Low-Lifes...... 5
Chapter 3:	Let Me Read That Over Before You Print It..... 9
Chapter 4:	Media Relations Is Like A Conduit, Not A Sewer.. 13
Chapter 5:	Stop The Presses, We Have A New Product 15
Chapter 6:	Desperate People Do Some Pretty Dumb Things... 19
Chapter 7:	Bending Over For A Client...Literally......... 23
Chapter 8:	Some Helpful Media Relations Guidelines..... 27
Chapter 9:	Never, Ever Lie To The Media (Unless You Are Sure You Won't Get Caught) 31
Chapter 10:	CEO Spelled Backward Is "Ego" 35
Chapter 11:	Holy Crap! The CEO Is Coming To Town!..... 39
Chapter 12:	Love The CEO Or You're Fired............... 41
Chapter 13:	It All Starts At The Top—Unfortunately....... 45
Chapter 14:	God Bless Our Founder, A Man Respected By All.. 49
Chapter 15:	Dealing With Different Media: Your Survival Rides On It 51
Chapter 16:	Making A Real Difference As A PR Puke 55
Chapter 17:	The Saga Of The Solar Phone: Leading-Edge Technology?..57

Chapter 18:	The Worst Coupon Ever To Appear In A Phone Directory..................................61
Chapter 19:	Other Crises: If You Want Sympathy, Die At Home......................................67
Chapter 20:	Not All Short People Have A Napoleonic Complex....................................71
Chapter 21:	Off Our Rockers Over Walter Cronkite.......75
Chapter 22:	We Have The Situation Completely Under Control—Almost............................77
Chapter 23:	When The Media Screw Up..................79
Chapter 24:	The Shame Of It All! Sucking Up To Influencers.................................83
Chapter 25:	"I Have A Collect Call From A Convict..."....87
Chapter 26:	Please, Lord, Not A Groundbreaking!........89
Chapter 27:	The Annual Report Cover From Hell.........93
Chapter 28:	"Leaving To Pursue Other Interests": His Butt Has Been Canned..........................97
Chapter 29:	The One Word That Causes Executive Urination..................................101
Chapter 30:	Let's Hold A Meeting, I Didn't Have Anything Better To Do.....................105
Chapter 31:	The Company's Designated "Pin Pimp"......109
Chapter 32:	Human Resources: Why Idiots Get Hired.....113
Chapter 33:	The Bobby Knight News Conference........117
Chapter 34:	The Only Place Where The Truth Is Told: The Men's Restroom......................121
Chapter 35:	Corporate Policies: Real Employee Ego-Boosters..............................125
Chapter 36:	Giving Birth To An Elephant: The Evaluation Process..................................127
Chapter 37:	Some Final Thoughts.....................131

CHAPTER

1

"Confessions Of A Corporate Sycophant"

Now, let's discuss the title of this book.

A good friend of mine (his name rhymes with Tom Rafferty) once remarked after a particularly worthless meeting that we are just corporate sycophants at a huge global conglomerate. I gave him that knowing, agreeable, nod and said, "Boy, you got that right."

We spoke some more and I soon realized he wasn't going to tip me off to what exactly a sycophant was. Dammit. It's like when you meet someone and can't remember who he is and you internally are begging him for help in identifying himself. I have had half-hour conversations with people and still don't remember who they are.

I discreetly scooted back to my cubicle to look the word "sycophant" up in my trusty American Heritage Dictionary.

A sycophant is defined as "a person who attempts to win favor or advance himself (obviously a sexist dictionary writer) by flattering persons of influence." In another section it notes, "a parasite of the rich or powerful and stresses self-seeking motives."

Yes, he did pretty much nail my job when he used the word "sycophant." Yes, most corporate communications people are corporate sycophants. Hey, we aren't the only ones by a long shot—we're just considered the best at it.

We tell the executives that they are great, they are all-knowledgeable, they walk on water, blah, blah, blah. We will proudly put that in a news release if they want and broadcast it to the world.

Our self-seeking motive for all this sycophanting (is that a real word?) is continuous employment. Our hope is that they don't actually start believing all the smoke we are blowing up their butts.

A vice president once told me, "No one ever tells the president of a company the truth." After decades in corporate life, I am convinced that statement is true. The truth will set you free—free to find another job.

The original title of this book was supposed to be **"Good Morning/Afternoon/Evening,"** but my book consultant (see wife) thought that was too confusing (as if using the word "sycophant" isn't confusing enough).

Let me tell the story behind that title.

I have written literally hundreds of speeches for executives at all levels. Some of my speeches were good, some were quite bad, and probably most of them were somewhere in-between. I never claimed to be Hemingway.

Writing a speech should be a very personal endeavor. You need to know your audience, your executive and what he/she hopes to accomplish in the allotted time period.

As a highly trained and respected speechwriter, you should sit down with the executive for several hours to finely hone the message. But good luck with that—in the real world it often boils down to "I have to give a speech to the Chamber next Tuesday about how great our company is. Get me a draft a few days ahead of time."

In some ways it is a compliment when an executive has confidence in your ability to deliver a quality speech with little or no direction. In other ways it can be scary. He is the one who has to stand in front of a group of several hundred people and not make a complete ass of himself.

Lest you ever forget, you learn quickly in PR that you will be blamed if his speech sucks. That is just the way the corporate world rolls…

Back to my story. I once had to write a speech for our top executive with very little input. In fact, I didn't even know what time of day he would be delivering it.

So I wrote the speech with this opening: "Good Morning/Afternoon/Evening." Obviously, as a CEO of a multinational company, I figured he could determine on his own whether it was morning, afternoon, or evening.

Big mistake.

You probably can guess the rest. He opened his speech by announcing proudly, "Good Morning, Afternoon, Evening…."

But, amazingly, thanks to the incompetence of my executive, his gaffe was unrecognized. He delivered the opening line while the audience was still clapping after his introduction and getting settled in their seats.

He could have just as well told them, "Good folks, you can kiss my executive butt," and they would have missed it.

The standard rule of speaking is to let your audience get settled and then begin your remarks. Luckily, my guy didn't seem to know that rule. Sometimes God watches over PR people. Thank you!

CHAPTER

2

Trying To Manage Those Media Low-Lifes

While we in media relations/public relations/communications are all lining up to kiss our executives' rosy red butts, the people in the media really don't have to.

In fact, most good reporters refuse to. That can be a problem.

As communications professionals, it is our role to "manage" those media low-lifers. As a former media low-life, it isn't always easy.

Throughout their entire lives, most executives are used to everyone kissing up to them. And in a corporation, this smooching thrives. Through ongoing study and implementation, I have found that 98.6 percent (people love percentages even if they are bogus) of all internal company publications (also known as house organs and useless pieces of doo-doo) are self-serving documents that are principally designed to flatter executives.

I have written, edited, and printed publications and have had to occasionally stop to laugh out loud at some of the stuff even I was putting in them. You sometimes think your fingers kind of smell from the BS you are writing.

In reality, many executives don't understand the distinction between an internal publication and the real-life outside journalistic media at newspapers, radio and TV stations. That can certainly cause problems if you are a PR guy trying to walk the tightrope between both worlds.

Rather than risk a real interview with a real reporter, many execs would prefer to simply have their own employees interview them for their own in-house publication. It certainly takes the guesswork out of whether a story will be positive or not when you are paying for it.

Here's a capsule summary of why most company-issued internal publications suck:

- They are designed to put a happy face on the company. Any employee who actually believes any of the information in one should undergo psychological testing.

- They enable executives' egos to run rampant. Hard-hitting stories like "Working Together to Achieve Our Goals," "Teamwork: The Key to Our Success," or my favorite, "Employees are our Greatest Asset," would normally induce employees to vomit. Fortunately, 99.9 percent of employees read the headline, chuckle and go on with their lives, thus saving numerous corporate barf-a-ramas.

- They are a power thing. Internal publications might be the most edited documents ever produced. I have seen a simple two-page article for an in-house publication be scrutinized by 30 people in an organization and rewritten literally for months.

- They show off writing excellence. Most of the people editing these publications normally couldn't write a two-paragraph memo that would make any sense. Executives and their sycophants edit the hell out of a story (often drafted by a professional writer) as if they actually know what they are doing. There is nothing greater than making one executive's changes only to have a second one completely rewrite the first one's masterpiece. And so on. (My record for a 10-paragraph story was one that was rewritten 16 times.)

- Executives can change history in their own publications. In fact, they can do an interview, go back and change their stupid quotes, add any pearls of wisdom they may have come across, or do whatever. They look on it as "This is *my* paper and I can say anything I want." They are correct. It really is their damn paper!

The bottom line is there are few documents as seldom read as an internal publication, but few that are as carefully edited, rewritten and analyzed. The vast majority of them make you feel genuinely sorry for the trees that were sacrificed in the process.

I've always felt that the process executives do in rewriting an internal publication is what we used to refer to in my younger days as a "circle jerk." Every young boy has heard of the circle jerk story; however, it is doubtful you will ever find anyone who actually participated in one.

The premise is that a group of young horny boys goes into a dark room and agrees to masturbate, with the first to reach nirvana declared the winner. The problem is that all the boys are playing a hoax on one dumb kid. When he masturbates and proclaims himself the winner, they turn on the light and everyone roars and makes fun of him for the rest of his life.

This is one of those classic mythological stories where no real human being has actually participated in a circle jerk, but everyone has heard a great story of someone who did.

Corporate life is the closest to a genuine "circle jerk" that most of us will ever experience. I often felt many of the executives I dealt with were the losers in the circle jerk game and were taking it out on the rest of humanity the rest of their lives because of it.

CHAPTER

3

Let Me Read That Over Before You Print It

Real problems can arise in a corporation when executives think that an external publication like a newspaper is the same as an internal one where they have total control. They sometimes forget that they don't own, control or pay legitimate news reporters.

There is nothing quite as embarrassing as an executive telling a "real" print reporter, "I'd like to read your story over before you publish it." It happens all the time, despite my always telling (begging) him/her not to ask that question.

And, if you are a reporter and say anything other than "It is against our policy to show a story to someone before we print it," then you should be shot. If you want some corporate jerk to edit your story, get a job at the corporation. I did.

Several years ago I called a reporter friend of mine to pitch him a story about how my firm—a worldwide engineering and construction company—built huge scale models of the facilities we were designing and constructing. Some of these models encompassed an entire room (or more), rose to 10 feet high, and were exact in every detail.

Once the models were constructed to exacting detail, they were shipped to the actual construction site and used as reference tools by the on-site workers. One reason for the models was to show clients exactly what their plant would look like when it was finished. Another reason was many construction workers didn't even know how to read a blueprint. We usually didn't mention that fact.

I knew the model story was a good feature story. Every guy has put together scale models in his lifetime. I didn't have to twist my reporter friend's arm to get him to come out and talk to our head model maker and his staffers.

I was confident that his feature piece would take the tone of how important these models were to construction and how unique our model builders were. I also figured the reporter was going to use the angle of how adults were now building models just like we did as kids.

After my reporter friend interviewed many of the model makers, the head model builder asked the reporter if he could see the story before it was published. I winced. I had told the model guy specifically *not* to ask that question. He did anyway.

Normally, my reporter friend would have given the standard "It is against our publication's policy to show an article to someone before it's published." However, since I was there and we were friends, unfortunately, he agreed to let us read it over before publication. Ugh.

A few days later the reporter sent his story to me. I read it, made just a few minor changes (edits that were unique to the engineering industry) and sent it to the model shop people to look over. Three days later they finally returned the story. They had completely rewritten the entire article. In fact, they even gave me their new copy of the story to give to my friend.

Suffice it to say that model builders are not exactly Hemingways. However, as one might expect, the version drafted by the model makers made them seem like brain surgeons who had constructed this marvelous piece of art through months of exacting work.

According to them, only a few chosen people in the world could have done what they had accomplished, but God gave them the talent to be model makers. In short, their version thoroughly sucked. It was laughable.

In the tradition of a true sycophant, I read the model makers' version over and told them their article was much better than my reporter friend's (BS). "Wow, you guys really improved his story," I said to further reinforce my lies. I told them I would definitely forward it to the reporter with my strong recommendation that he run their edited version "as is."

But this is where I really proved my worth as a communicator. I warned my modelers that although their story was the equivalent of "War and Peace," sometimes "these damn reporters" get defensive when their stories are rewritten. He might not use their superb version, but I would try my level best to convince him otherwise.

Then I promptly took the rewritten story done by the model makers and tossed it in the garbage. I sent the reporter back his original story with my minor edits and told him it was great as is. "Our model shop people thought it was wonderful and really captured the essence of their jobs," I told him.

I then told the model shop people that the reporter liked their version (which I had trashed) better than his own. I did caution them that sometimes "editors get a little defensive about changing their reporters' stories and the publication might still use the original story."

The reporter's original story ran with my minor edits. Although it was not the rewritten version our model makers had supplied the reporter, they eventually determined that maybe his article was "okay."

The bottom line to all this is that reporters should never let anyone see a story before it is printed. It sure would have saved me a lot of time, effort and lying. Amen.

CHAPTER

4

Media Relations Is Like A Conduit, Not A Sewer

Early in my communications career, a wise and crusty PR guy, let's call him "Syd" (a former Associated Press journalist), told me that "media relations should be like a conduit, not a sewer." As is typical when someone says something profound, I wholeheartedly agreed and then asked him exactly what he meant by that statement (see "sycophant").

"When you want to work with reporters the relationship had better go both ways, like a conduit," Syd said. "When you want to pitch a story to reporters, let them know what the news value is. If it's good, they'll do a story on it. If not, they'll let you know."

Then he stressed the sewer aspect. "Don't call a reporter regularly to hype stuff, but then not call him back when he needs something from you," he said. "In other words, your relationship with reporters should not be one where the crap all goes one way."

Syd has since gone to the great ink factory in the sky, but his words have stuck with me for twenty-five years. And, in my experience, he was right on target.

I have heard media relations people ask reporters to do a story on their CEO "because he's a really neat guy and genuinely cares about the people in his organization." However, when the same reporter has a question about a company executive who stole $20 million from the company, the PR person hides under his desk.

If you are going to be a media relations pro, you have to handle the not-so-great with the good. That's where you earn your spurs. You have to take the good with the bad.

With a former business reporter I dealt with, if you failed to return a call to him—just once—you could forget him ever doing a story on your company unless the news item was absolutely too big to pass up. You did not want to get on his poop list.

He would give speeches to such groups as the Public Relations Society of America and the International Association of Business Communicators and scare the hell out of them. When he would bellow, "The crap had better go both ways if you plan on dealing with me," half the crowd would pee in their pants.

CHAPTER

5

Stop The Presses, We Have A New Product

Sometimes the media simply don't understand the pressure put on PR types to get the company name on TV, radio or in newspapers. Every time the company comes out with anything new, the executives expect the news media to drop everything and breathlessly announce the new product or service.

Remember, we aren't talking paid ads, but free editorial copy. I sometimes felt our executives thought the media were waiting breathlessly by their phones for me to call them and say, "Good news, Bill, our new bar of soap is a bathing breakthrough and you can do a story about it!"

Executives think the process works this way: They come over to your desk and say that the company is introducing a new product.

"We need to get some great publicity on it," they add.

Now, from a practical point of view, the product might really be a piece of crap that another company introduced five years ago and your company is now copying it. However, to your executive, that is irrelevant.

Your executive then envisions a headline about the same size as the one that read "WAR ENDS IN JAPAN" that would say "ACME ANNOUNCES NEW PRODUCT."

In your article, it should also quote him extensively, saying such memorable things as "We think our product will revolutionize the industry. It is state-of-the-art and will dramatically change the course of the world. Customers can write us at xxxx Broadway or call us at 444-3432."

The executive thinks that accomplishing this task simply takes a phone call by the PR puke to the newspaper. Upon receiving the call, the reporter is breathlessly supposed to say, "Stop the presses! I've got the ACME PR guy on the phone and his company is coming out with a new product!"

The executive thinks this happens this way because he saw a black and white movie made in 1932 about the newspaper business, and that's how the media acted. Of course, I think that movie involved the death penalty, but that's not important to him.

In reality, you call the newspaper and get the reporter's voice mail eight straight times.

You finally get through and breathlessly explain your company's new product. That is followed by an awkward silence from the reporter's end that says, in essence, "Pardon me, but you are getting me mixed up with someone who gives a rat's ass about your product."

Upon hearing your desperate new product pitch/whine, the reporter might respond with "Send me a news release on it." This, in essence, means that he wants to get off the phone and figures your sending him a release might buy him some time instead of telling you "no" right on the phone.

Savvy reporters know I can buy time by telling my executives that "I think the reporter is interested. I sent him the release…."

At this point a good PR person might have to resort to tried-and-true tricks of the trade. If you have nude pictures of the reporter's mother, sister or wife, this might be a good time to remind him about them.

If you picked up the tab for golf, dinner, drinks, anything, you might want to mention it. In other words, your ass is going to be in a sling if this is not in the paper soon. You sometimes gotta do what you gotta do….

CHAPTER

6

Desperate People Do Some Pretty Dumb Things

I would like to say that I have always acted with the highest scruples in dealing with the media. Yes, I would like to say that, but sometimes…

True story. I was called into an executive's office on a Thursday and was told that I was expected to get our company in the news over the weekend.

Why? Because my boss had been bragging about me to other executives and said she could guarantee "John can get media coverage for our company this weekend."

I told her I would certainly try to do that. She then told me she wasn't suggesting it, she was telling me to handle it or consider searching for a new job. I felt like I was part of some stupid bet she had made since I had been recently promoted.

My challenge was simple: Get publicity that shows our company as caring, or lose my job. It made me feel proud to work for such a group of numb-nuts.

I asked our community relations people if we were involved in anything over the weekend. When they said the March of Dimes' famous WalkAmerica event, I was ecstatic. This was an annual event where hundreds of our employees walked to raise money for the March of Dimes.

However, our "caring company" used to give employees T-shirts as a way of saying thanks for participating, but had stopped doing that because of cost considerations. A $12 billion company saved $5 on a T-shirt. It meant the number of employees participating had dropped off significantly.

It is not a very positive story when your company had 3,000 walkers one year and now only has 1,800. In fact, there was no real way to spin it positively. I was desperate.

I checked and found out that a local TV station and its main anchor was covering the event "live" and I tried to figure out how I could get our company on that broadcast.

Did I say I was desperate?

If there is one trait common to virtually everyone on TV, it's that they have huge egos. Let's face it, they spend their life looking into a camera and being recognized by fans. It takes a big ego to do the job successfully.

I called the PR person for the TV station and told her that "our employees would like to thank your anchorperson for his dedication to the community and present him with the "Acme Company Award for Community Service." Let me add, he would be the first non-company person to ever receive this prestigious award."

She was ecstatic! Anytime a TV anchorperson can be portrayed as a nice, community-minded person, the ratings go up. I promptly went out and had a plaque created. Yes, the anchor was the first non-employee to ever to receive the Acme Company Award for Community Service. In fact, he was the ***only*** person to ever receive the award, since it had been created simply for the on-air TV presentation.

In the end, everyone was happy. The anchor loved receiving the award. Our executive was thrilled to be on TV. And I got to keep my job.

Kind of a win-win-win thing...

CHAPTER

7

Bending Over For A Client...Literally

Television health reporters are a strange lot. They are generally female and are often not a real part of the newsroom. Some do their two-minute "Fruits are good, fat is bad" segments and go home.

Many are fed their stories by local hospitals or via video news releases issued by drug companies. "VNRs," as they are called, are video segments produced entirely by companies and sent to reporters and editors.

Although many TV stations proclaim they never use VNRs, most do. What a VNR does is allow a reporter to simply follow a script written by the company with the visuals already provided. It is designed to make the reporter look like he/she has developed the story when in reality it was provided to sell a company's product or service.

The key to a successful VNR is that you cannot make it look too damn obvious that you are pimping your product. You can put your company's name and have your spokesperson quoted, but it simply cannot come across as an advertisement.

Back to health reporters. Luckily I rarely have had to deal with them. Most only seem to want to focus on women's health issues: "Breast Exams are Important" since that is a key demographic for TV stations

I was working with a health care client and had a perfect story for a "Health Watch" segment. I called one reporter and was told she only does stories on women between certain ages. Since my story involved men, she was not the least bit interested.

I called another Health Watch reporter and pitched the story. I could tell she didn't give a damn about it. I was irritated. I told her that there is more to health than having regular mammograms or the occasional silly story about prostate exams. I told her no one pays attention to them anymore.

"Well, John, when was the last time you had a prostate exam?" she asked. I told her I had never had one. It was the truth.

"I'll tell you what," she said. "If you get a prostate exam I will do your story."

Desperate people do desperate things. "You're on," I said. To be completely honest, I didn't even know what a prostate exam was. I thought it might be the famous "cough to the left" routine. Hey, I didn't go to med school.

So I called "my" doctor and scheduled the damn prostate exam. Actually, since I hadn't seen a doctor in a few years, "my" doctor was selected because he was close to my home. If I am going to have my testicles juggled, I might as well use a doctor in the area.

I went to my appointment and sat in the waiting room for a full hour. I was irritated. I was ushered into a tiny examination room, and after about 15 minutes the doctor walked in, looking at my chart the whole time.

"I see here, Mr. Landsberg, you are here for a prostate exam," he read. "Are you having any problems?"

I was honest. I explained that I was a PR person and pitched a story and was having my prostate (whatever the hell that is) examined so my client's story might air.

"You're kidding," he said.

"Not at all," I replied.

At that point he gave me a little smirk and started putting on a rubber glove and putting some solution on it. He told me to drop my pants. I knew I was screwed–literally.

I think he stuck his finger, a log and then his entire arm up my butt. Okay, maybe I exaggerated a bit, but that was the sensation. It was the kind of thing guys fear might happen to them in prison.

He gave me a clean bill of health. I went home and asked my wife if she knew what was involved with a prostate exam. She did. She thought it was hilarious. I didn't.

I called the "Health Watch" reporter and let her know that, per our agreement, I had let some person I just met violate me rectally. She chuckled.

"I didn't think it was that funny," I told her. "And when can I set up the interview with my client?"

There was silence on the other end of the line. "I will have to check with my editor if we can do the story," she said calmly.

To me that was basically her telling me that not only did the doctor stick stuff up my butt, but I could also put my story idea there.

"Wait a second," I said. "We had an agreement."

"Well, I have to run it past my editor," she said. I knew I was screwed. When reporters say they need to run a story past their editor, they are going to use the editor excuse to kill it. She never did the story.

I always thought I should have billed the client and even the damn TV station for what I went through pitching that story. "Medical expenses: $500 for reaming."

As far as I am concerned, "Health Watch" reporters can literally kiss my butt.

CHAPTER

8

Some Helpful Media Relations Guidelines

Years ago, I worked at a harness racing track in Cleveland. This was rather unique since I had never gone to the track prior to taking the job and had virtually no interest in horse racing.

As I progressed through my career, I also noticed that I really had no interest in greeting cards, engineering or telecom before joining companies that were involved in those endeavors.

At the racetrack, I did have an opportunity to work with Gail Egan, whom I still consider the best PR man I ever had the opportunity to work with. He's been dead for a number of years now, but I still thank him for the lessons he taught me.

Gail was a throwback to an earlier era. He smoked a stinky cigar, his car was so dirty and filled with press packets and clippings that if he opened the rear doors the stuff would literally fall out, and his sport coats were about 20 years behind the times.

Gail knew everyone in the Cleveland media—and I mean everyone.

Gail's main focus was the racetrack and publicizing events there, but he also did freelance PR for the Harlem Globetrotters when they came to town, as well as for boxing matches and "professional" wrestling.

When Gail would walk through the newsroom at The Plain Dealer in Cleveland, it was reminiscent of when Norm walked into the "Cheers" bar in the TV sitcom, only everyone yelled "Gail!" when he strolled in. Although much of his focus was on sports activities, Gail made a point of knowing reporters on all kinds of beats.

When I asked him why he spent so much time with the society editor, movie reviewers, education writers and the like, he said, "John, you never know when you might need them." He was right.

If one of his wrestlers happened to have a master's degree, Gail might pitch that story idea to the education writer. If the racetrack honchos were involved in a charity event, he would likely pitch it to the society editor. And, in doing so, he was exposing the events to wider audiences who might not read just the sports page.

I have found that many media relations practitioners focus only on those specific reporters who cover their specific beats (who they feel can "help them") and ignore the rest. If a major paper has a real estate reporter and that's your industry, it is fine to deal with him or her. Just don't limit yourself to that person.

You should also keep in mind that it is much more difficult to impress a reporter who knows your industry and deals in your industry every day. With reporters who are not experts in your field, you can pitch a variety of human-interest-type stories and achieve great success. If you're an education reporter who has to deal with school superintendents and principals day in and day out, it is nice to do a story about a company's in-house training.

Also, it is very difficult to lie to a reporter who specializes in your industry. In the long-distance-calling arena, it is very easy for a reporter to call a competitor and get the "real" story, so you have to be very careful. However, if you are with a long distance company and pitching a real estate story, you can lie all day and frequently not get caught.

In order not to get caught lying to the media, you have to at least use some common sense. There are lies, and then there are *lies!*

As an example, when Liberace died, his sycophants immediately said the cause was everything but AIDS. Of course, except for some aborigines living on the far reaches of the planet, everyone who read or heard that lie collectively groaned.

You see, the rule is *"When lying, at least be somewhere in the ballpark."* I will cover this theory more in-depth in the next chapter.

Gail also taught me a valuable lesson in the importance of localizing stories. We would develop unique stories about harness racing drivers and pitch them to their hometowns. Then we'd do stories on horse owners and send specific releases to their hometowns or where their businesses where located. I asked him once why we are we promoting owners and drivers. Gail just responded, "As long as they run the name of the racetrack in the story I really don't care what else a reporter uses."

Another thing Gail stressed to me was always to be loyal to the product you were promoting. I tried for years to get him to admit that "professional" wrestling was fake. He never would.

He would skirt the issue by telling stories about how local hot-shot wrestlers would try to take on legends such as "Bo Bo Brazil" and the like and how they would suffer greatly for their indiscretion. Gail knew he was selling a myth, but loyalty always prevailed with him.

Racetracks seem to attract strange people. I met one local boxing promoter and told Gail he seemed to be a pretty nice guy who tipped kids $20 to bring his car around after the races.

Gail gave me a paternal look. "John, he is paying them because there might be a bomb in his car and he wants them to blow up rather than him."

At the racetrack I often saw things that were not so pretty. After a long night of racing I would do radio broadcasts of the race results to a variety of stations and finish a few hours after the final race.

I'd walk down from the press box high above the track and see fans still sitting in their seats crying because they had lost everything. These were sick people with gambling problems and I rationalized it that if they didn't lose their money with us, they'd lose it somewhere else.

Hey, maybe they would have....

CHAPTER

9

Never, Ever Lie To The Media (Unless You Are Sure You Won't Get Caught)

All, and I mean all, books on corporate communications and media relations stress never, ever to lie to the media. While generally I agree with that axiom, I also think the caveat "when you can obviously get caught" should be added to that statement.

Media relations practitioners all stand in front of groups and say they "never, ever would lie to the media." What a bunch of crap. I would say fully 90 percent of the things I promoted resulted in lying in various degrees to the media.

As an example, a senior executive called me in and said that his wife was studying to be a minister and commuted each week to Chicago to a seminary there. He said it would be neat for me to notify the local paper and they could "do a story about how I have had to take care of the kids during the week. Kind of a 'Mr. Mom' kind of article."

In reality, he traveled frequently, and if he spent two hours a week with his family, that was a lot. His secretary dealt more with his family than he did.

However, I called the religion editor at the newspaper and pitched the story to her that "he's really a great guy (he wasn't) and cooks (his kids did) and cleans the house (he had a maid). I said his wife is very nice (when I spoke to her, I was glad I wasn't the same religion as her) and a caring person (other executive wives said the only person she cared for was herself).

So, after I lied so much my nose was sticking out about a foot, the nice religion editor said it sounded like a wonderful story and she would follow up. She did a wonderful story where three photos appeared. People who worked with the executive laughed at the total misrepresentation, but you do what you gotta do in PR.

During my career as a sycophant I often have had to come up with great pronouncements to show that our company "cared about each and every employee," that our "service to our customers was the envy of the industry" and so on. A friend of mine once proclaimed that I was the king of "foo-foo dust," meaning I would throw sparklers of BS on every situation.

Sadly, PR practitioners have to lie almost daily. And if the word "lie" offends you, maybe "overhype" is more appropriate. I could give a thousand examples, but let me talk about a few.

One of the greatest marketing events in the history of the world was the Gulf Crisis. This was a chance for corporate America to show that it "supported our troops" in their time of need and that they "cared." Cut me a break. corporate America "cares" about profits and bonuses. Anything else is pretty worthless to them.

Never, Ever Lie To The Media (Unless You Are Sure You Won't Get Caught)

The War gave us a chance to promote products and services. It was somewhat ironic hearing politicians and many of our executives explaining how we had to take a hard line and go into Kuwait and "kick some Iraqi ass."

One could probably count on one hand how many top executives ever served in the military. The vast majority of them spent their youth avoiding the draft for fear of going to Vietnam. They either had doctor friends get them medical deferments or they spent a decade at an Ivy League school until the draft ended.

However, the Mideast affair really brought out the new hardliners. Actually, Iraq picked the wrong country to invade. Not only did Kuwait have oil reserves and riches beyond belief, the country had also retained the famed PR firm of Hill & Knowlton to encourage U.S. support and involvement.

Pretty soon stories of Kuwaiti babies being tossed out of incubators were being highlighted in the U.S. media. The U.S. public was outraged. The fact that these stories were untrue and were placed by a PR agency made little difference.

My job was to get my telecom in the news. This was particularly difficult since the troops were in Saudi Arabia and we had no service from there to the U.S. Our competitors had set up calling stations in Saudi and tried to pretend they were helping the troops when actually many were charging the hell out of the soldiers.

I set up numerous conference calls, special Military Affiliates Radio System calls (short wave) and even worked with a nice lady to sing greetings to servicepeople's wives, all in the name of publicity. There were other things, but basically we fared very well and spent very little money.

We offered free conference calls to troops knowing they could probably never have the time to use them. Heck, if they did, they had to use our competitor's lines to get to us since we didn't really have the international service!

The timing for the end of the crisis was perfect. So many companies had provided so much crap to the military that the media were refusing to give them a plug. The general public was getting bored by the whole thing. I'm an Army veteran, and I was getting bored by it all.

I was sick of people who were constantly calling me and saying, "I just want to do something for our guys over there." They all could have added "and if I happen to make a few bucks on it, so be it."

As an example, one T-shirt vendor called and offered to do free T-shirts for all the troops in Saudi Arabia. And, he would let my company underwrite the venture at "his cost" for just $12 a shirt. Cut me a break. His cost was probably $2.

Another guy offered to put on seminars around the country for spouses of servicemen and my company could pay for them for about $7,000 each. The cost varied depending on how many people did the "fire walk."

Yep, he was planning on having the seminar attendees conclude the evening by walking on hot coals. I like to play practical jokes, but I held back the urge to send this proposal to the Legal Department.

All in all, the war was fascinating, but I was glad to see it end. These marketing endeavors can only run so long before people lose interest. I know I did.

CHAPTER

10

CEO Spelled Backward Is "Ego"

During my career I have had the unique opportunity to work under a variety of chief executive officers (CEOs). These are the top bananas in a corporation, and these men (sorry, ladies, there's not much room in that rarified air for women) have egos second to none.

While a handful actually worked their way from the bottom to the top (see "Mailroom to Boardroom": check under "Fantasy" on Google), the vast majority have attended private schools their whole lives. They can no more relate to an average employee than a white Southerner can relate to an African tribesman.

In school these future corporate leaders were the kids who got good grades, were pulled out of school for extended trips to Europe (Daddy just happened to be going there on business and could bury the trip in his expense account) and joined the right groups, i.e., Cub Scouts, Boys Scouts, Eagle Scouts, National Honor Society, etc.

These chosen ones did papers on "What's Good about American Business" and "God Bless the Free Enterprise System." The local Rotary and Kiwanis Clubs gave them the "Good Young Citizen of the Year" awards.

In college they went to prep schools. If they couldn't get into an Ivy League school despite daddy's money and pull (which meant they were really stupid), then they went to private liberal arts schools.

At one corporation where I worked, the CEO assigned one of the company's writers to crank out a term paper for his son. Luckily, the kid got an "A" on the paper since the writer would likely have lost his job if any other grade was awarded. Talk about pressure!

Basically, in college, future CEOs acted like the ROTC officer in the movie "Animal House." He was the guy who wore the shiny helmet and bossed people around. Generally, a Master's degree followed since it looks better on a resume.

Upon graduation the future CEO joined a company as a "management trainee," "executive assistant" or some other special position. These titles mean "I am being fast-tracked. My father is a CEO somewhere and I am being groomed for big things. Do not get on my wrong side. Although I have been in this corporation three days and am not even sure where the men's room is, I can ruin your life if you give me a hard time."

It's easy to be jealous of these young snots. They've never had a really crappy job like busing tables, washing cars or delivering newspapers. Heck, they've never even had to fill out a job application or interview with some guy who has you down as the 14th interview he's done today for the position, and he's got eight more to go. Personnel people just "take care of" these special people.

And, unless this future CEO does something really stupid like kill some employees (probation, at best), he's steadily moved through the organization. If he moves every one to two years into a new position, then he never is really accountable for any screw-ups along the way.

After 10 years of "positions of increasing responsibility," which was my favorite expression in news releases to mean he's held a series of jobs in various departments with handpicked titles, he is now the CEO. This is where problems begin and the ego kicks into turbocharge.

As CEO, you are responsible for relating to the "little people" at your company. That's not easy when the closest you ever were to "little people" was to the maid, gardener and daddy's chauffeur. There aren't a lot of classes in college dealing with "Motivating Common People" or "How to get People to Produce without Actually Having to Touch or Talk to Them."

Not all CEOs are aloof and insensitive about what makes employees' tick. I've met maybe a handful in my career who weren't.

CHAPTER

11

Holy Crap! The CEO Is Coming To Town!

When the CEO of your corporation decides to visit your small subsidiary, it is a big deal. It rarely happens, and everyone from the top down moves into advanced suck-up mode.

The CEO of our corporation announced he was going to give an update to our executive staffers on the health of the entire organization. We were told he would be arriving on a Friday via the corporate jet, and we were supposed to have a special van available for his use for the weekend.

The schedule involved the CEO flying into our airport, with our president picking him up and taking him to a hotel ballroom, where he would update our staffers on corporate happenings.

My job was to take our special corporate van and meet the pilot, and we would unload some personal items. I was then supposed to take the van to the hotel and get the keys to the CEO for him to use for the weekend.

When I met the pilot he seemed irritated as hell. We began unloading the plane and it was stuff like lamps, crappy tables, books, etc. Most of it looked like something for a dorm room.

"What is this crap?" I asked the pilot.

"He's taking his spoiled brat kid back to college," muttered the pilot. "That's the only reason he is here today. He's giving your executives an update only so he can use the corporate jet and your van for free."

After the weekend I looked out my window and saw the company van in the parking lot. The rear bumper looked like it had hooked on to something and was pointing in the wrong direction.

"John, the CEO wrecked the damn van," said our safety guy. "We want you to say you were driving it and wrecked it."

I declined. Fake accident reports were a big thing and I didn't trust that our safety guy wouldn't screw me later over it. He found someone else to take the blame.

When the dust finally settled, it sure took away the luster from our CEO visiting us.

CHAPTER

12

Love The CEO Or You're Fired

Unfortunately, many CEOs think they can simply write a letter to employees in the internal house organ telling them what assets they are, or even mention them in the annual report (true words from God), and that will keep them happy.

However, employees are somewhat skeptical of both these methods. They often like to see their top executives on a regular basis and even communicate with them occasionally.

I once was in an executive meeting loosely titled "Improving the CEO's Image with Employees." Our goal was to "humanize" the CEO with employees.

This came about because the CEO had earlier agreed to participate in thanking employees for strong quarterly financial results by standing at an entrance in the morning and greeting them as they came to work. The idea bombed.

We never actually thought he would participate in this venture, but he surprised us by showing up. Unfortunately, most employees walked in and thought two things:

1. The CEO was taking attendance and checking when everyone got to work.
2. Who the hell is this guy by the door thanking us for a good quarter?

Basically, employees who recognized him were scared of him. Others didn't know who the hell he was. Either way, the CEO sensed he was not portraying the friendly image he desired.

During the meeting, I felt somewhat radical and suggested some ideas for the CEO to do to relate to employees.

"Why don't we have him go to lunch in the employee cafeteria!" I said.

One of the VPs gave me a look that would kill and said, "He would never eat with employees."

Then I said, "Why not have the CEO just kind of walk around the office during the day? Kind of like the theory of 'Managing by Walking Around' that is popular today?"

Again, I got "the look" that said my idea sucked.

"He hates to just walk around and talk with employees," replied the VP. "I'm certainly not going to suggest he do that."

In corporate life, you learn quickly that if you have two suggestions and both have been shoved up your butt, you generally should low-key your presence from that point on. Two strikes and you're way behind in the count. Three and you are job searching.

But I was feeling bold and thought I would try one more suggestion for humanizing the CEO in the mind of employees.

"Mother's Day is around the corner and many of our female employees have to work that day," I said. "Why not have the CEO bring in donuts and treats for them to say thanks for their efforts? I could even get some good media coverage for it."

It was like I had suggested that the CEO strip down naked in front of shareholders. My wonderful ideas all fell flat. I was crushed.

The meeting concluded with a suggestion that the company donate some money to a cause and put the CEO's name on it, that we use his photo more in internal publications (the old record was 11 times in one publication) and that we use him in a video message to employees.

Yep, I'm damn proud to report that our challenge was to improve his image to employees. And when the dust cleared from our meeting, the CEO was not going to have to go near any one of those scumbags.

It made me proud to be in meetings like that.

CHAPTER

13

It All Starts At The Top—Unfortunately

PR people are probably the ultimate sycophants, but just about everyone else in the organization falls into that category whether they want to admit it or not. The CEO, president, general manager—whatever you call the top person—of every company in America sets the tone for that whole organization.

Every management book in the world written since the 1800s always recommends that worker bees "should always dress like your boss."

That way, in theory, if you're lucky enough to have a boss who has a fatal accident, then key Human Resource people will say, "Gee, John always dressed the part of his boss, let's promote him into that spot once we've buried good old whatshisname."

It is this type of mind-set that rules corporate America today and will probably continue this way for centuries to come. "Heck, if the CEO believes that, then if I want to be CEO someday I'd better do likewise" is a common mantra taught to employees.

Sometimes I didn't realize how far this could be taken. I was speaking to a vice president one time and he mentioned that George, a real fast-tracker corporate sycophant extraordinaire, was really doing all the right things to get ahead.

"He even belongs to the right church," the VP said with pride in his voice. I asked what church that was, and he mentioned some Episcopal church in town where "everybody who is anybody goes, including the CEO."

I went home dismayed. I told my wife that for 30 years we had been attending the wrong church, and I asked her if she would be terribly upset if I would give up Catholicism. As wives often are, she was not very understanding.

This phenomenon was clearly evident at one job where the CEO would leave every Friday afternoon around 3 p.m. If you went down to the executive wing around 2:45 p.m., the execs were so busy it looked like they would have to work around the clock all weekend to complete their tasks.

You could hear shouts of "If it takes all weekend to complete that report on lawn maintenance, well, by God, we'll be here." Or "Mr. Big (CEO) said we had better examine that issue, so we're all staying here until it is properly examined."

When the CEO left at 3 p.m., within 10 minutes his staffers were gone. It never failed.

The CEO affects all facets of corporate life. If he drinks like a fish, his reportees will do likewise. If he cheats on his wife, then it is okay for everyone else to fool around. Employees always try to figure out what he wants and respond appropriately.

At one organization we had special electronic cards we used with the doors that showed when we came in the office and went.

It All Starts At The Top—Unfortunately

Our CEO was a workaholic, so on Saturdays and Sundays our department designated one person to take all our cards and sign in with them. It made us look like we all worked 60 hours a week.

We were so proud of our tactic. When the CEO left to take another position, I asked him if he actually checked the work hours of employees. He didn't even know we monitored it.

If a newspaper article lambasted the company terribly, we would say the article wasn't as positive as we would have liked, but that "if not for our damage control with the reporter, it was going to be much worse."

In essence, the article sucked, but we told others if not for us it would have been worse. So much for the truth….

CHAPTER

14

God Bless Our Founder, A Man Respected By All

I once worked at a greeting card company (not Hallmark, but real close) that was owned and run by some of the cheapest people I have ever met. Most top executives will spend money on themselves like drunken sailors since it's generally "company" money, which doesn't really count to them. These guys owned the company and were tightwads.

The founder was about 130-years-old and the company still boasted that he worked regular hours each day. Actually, his chauffer brought him in the morning and he slept most of the time, but hell, if I had his millions, I never would have come to work.

Around 11 o'clock each day the old guy would begin his daily trek to the executive cafeteria. In his younger days it probably would have taken him about five minutes. Now, it took him about 45.

The first time I saw him on the luncheon voyage, it amazed me how he stopped every few steps, bent over, picked something up, and went on. He paid little or no attention to employees as they said "hi" to him (his hearing wasn't the greatest), but he looked down all the time and performed this little ritual.

After about a week on the job, I found out what this little ritual was about. The founder couldn't stand the thought that a paper clip might be wasted and religiously picked up each one he found on the floor on his way to lunch.

I later saw an employee walking down the hall purposely dropping paper clips on the floor.

Yes, our illustrious founder wouldn't give employees the time of day. But they got their revenge every day watching him picking the paper clips up.

CHAPTER

15

Dealing With Different Media: Your Survival Rides On It

As I mentioned earlier, working with the media is my cup of tea. I have been doing it for about 25 years and it still excites me. Of course, each medium is unique, and you have to know some of the tricks of the trade in dealing with each one.

PRINT—The print media are still the key media in the world today despite massive layoffs of some superb journalists. If you can get a good story placed in a key publication, the remaining media will follow like lemmings. This is because print journalists often have specific beats and develop contacts over a period of time. Contrast that with the tenure of an average TV assignment editor, which is about a week, or a radio newscaster, which is about three days, and you can see the edge a newspaper reporter has.

When pitching a story, always pitch it first to a newspaper reporter and let him/her determine whether it is newsworthy. If he/she thinks it is stupid, he/she will generally tell you, and then you can pitch it to a TV station or, lastly, a radio station.

While many people today will say TV is the most powerful medium (which it probably is), in business life a good newspaper story takes precedence. Why? Because you can route it to all the executives and get brownie points!

If you route a TV video clip to executives, most will never take the time to view it. You can route a transcript of a TV or radio broadcast, but they appear very skimpy on a piece of paper and executives value a story by its length.

Keep in mind, unless the executive staff sees a positive clip about your company, you don't receive any credit for your effort. If you don't receive credit, you'll find Human Resources calling soon.

I admit I am biased toward print reporters since I used to be one. Like many reporters, I made the jump from the legitimate press to the illegitimate press, which is what corporate PR positions are often labeled. They got bylines. I got money.

Print reporters assume you are lying to them at all times. Since you generally are, this is a correct assumption on their part. The key is to have a relationship where the print reporter will call you for information and you will call him back.

I would say fully 90 percent of the companies today receive negative publicity for one key reason: They deserve it! I have heard people in media relations whine that the local paper doesn't like their company or "they have it in for us." What a bunch of crap!

I can't tell you how many times I have called a reporter back after receiving a phone message and have had them exclaim: "Gee, thanks for getting back to me." I always tell them that's my job, but they say "PR people never return calls."

Going back to my conduit vs. sewer analogy, this is why reporters have it in for your stupid company. They are so frustrated getting responses to any of their questions that they avoid the PR person and talk to other sources—like employees—who will often be honest, which is not a desirable trait in a corporation.

TV Reporters—In many cases, the words "TV journalism" are an oxymoron. Unless you have something visually exciting, it is not considered a story on TV, which eliminates a lot of newsworthy stories. Many TV anchor people, for the most part, are grown-up Barbie and Ken dolls.

A recent consultant's report on a Kansas City TV station was leaked to the press and the subsequent story talked about how anchor people should look longer at each other (lovingly?) after a story, how they should give those happy grins and "act sincere" when a story like an airplane going down is broadcast. Print reporters love stories like that about their TV counterparts.

Radio Reporters—It is tough to trash radio reporters since many stations have only one reporter and it is his/her job to cover every news event within 100 miles. Most are relegated to "ripping and reading" copy from The Associated Press or stealing directly from the local newspaper or "USA Today."

Journalists today have changed. In their search for some glitzy exposé, they frequently miss the real news. This is particularly true in corporations, where they will do a stupid piece on smoking in the workplace while 500 employees are working on a project to merge the company with another.

Unfortunately, it is much easier to do the smoking story, so don't expect any big journalistic shift in the future.

CHAPTER

16

Making A Real Difference As A PR Puke

Sometimes it is difficult as a PR professional (or PR Puke as some executives like to call us) to make a real difference in an organization. At times we have to consider minor victories in our quest to be loved and appreciated.

One of my greatest successes involved the men's restroom at our corporate headquarters. It was your normal restroom, but it had a series of urinals without those little privacy walls between them.

For some reason I don't even understand today, I really wanted the privacy walls.

I asked the maintenance guys if they would put up the walls. "When I am standing there peeing, other guys look over and they feel inadequate," I joked. They ignored me.

When we got a new maintenance guy, I tried again for privacy walls. He ignored me.

I even anonymously filled out a suggestion card for privacy walls. Ignored. My three-year quest was failing miserably.

It was announced that we were going to have our annual shareholders meeting at corporate headquarters. I noticed our maintenance guys painted and recarpeted and even added pictures wherever the shareholders might go before and after the meeting.

I saw my opportunity and took it. I told the maintenance guy that privacy walls in the men's room would be a very good idea for shareholders. I kind of hinted that the CEO had suggested it. Okay, I said it was the CEO's idea.

The walls were put up the next day. It may have been my largest corporate accomplishment.

CHAPTER

17

The Story Of The Solar Phone: Leading-Edge Technology?

First, let me stress that while public relations people are generally excellent liars, that title always goes to sales and marketing folks in a corporation. Not only do they lie about their products and services to every external audience they meet, they also lie to co-workers. Hell, they probably lie to themselves.

Lying to co-workers is not good. It is kind of like when I was in the Army. Nobody cared if you stole 50 tanks, 400 rifles, 250 hand grenades, 500 bayonets and the general's jeep. However, you better not steal a sock from another enlisted man or you could get killed. One kind of stealing was from the Army and nobody cared; the other was just not right and could really get you in deep doo-doo.

It's kind of like that in companies. Nobody cares what a salesperson tells a customer to get a sale: "Sir, I really think if you push the right buttons this telephone will perform oral sex on you."

However, sales and marketing types then go to us PR types and say, "You know, if you push the right buttons, this telephone will perform oral sex on you. How about developing a press release and sending it out?" We immediately are leery of such a suggestion.

This was the case for the first and only solar pay telephone enclosure ever installed in the great State of Ohio. It was back in May 1983 and was a classic example of a marketer getting a PR person to hype something that was a piece of crap.

Our illustrious Marketing Department folks had done considerable research and found that only six states had ever used solar power to light an outside telephone booth. It was just to light the damn phone booth. That was all. The actual phone service was handled via normal copper wires like any other pay phone.

The six states were all in warm climates like Florida, Texas, Arizona, and the like. This was the first time it was ever tried in Ohio, but we were confident this was the first of many solar phone booths, and our company was damn proud to be a pacesetter in this new technology.

The media loved it. The only problem was many of them thought that not only did it light the pay phone; it also somehow helped provide phone service. When one TV reporter noted that even on cloudy days the phone worked perfectly, I almost puked, but thought it might be best not to correct him.

In reality, the actual phone would work perfectly in total darkness forever! Only the little light bulb lighting the damn thing would be out of commission.

Not only did that TV story go nationwide, but even an encyclopedia used a photo of it to show some of the high-tech things telecommunications companies were doing. Our marketing folks were ecstatic with the coverage.

The Story Of The Solar Phone: Leading-Edge Technology?

Within a month the solar pay phone light was dying. Although it could store electricity for up to 5.7 days, Ohio's cloudiness was killing it.

As one of my friends from Florida remarked shortly after relocating to Ohio, "The sun never shines in this damn state." He was right.

On top of a humongous lack of sun, our brilliant marketers soon discovered that the famous solar phone booth also didn't operate in temperatures below 30 degrees. In Ohio, that means it would be out of commission about 90 percent of the time. It's below that temperature in July in Ohio!

Within six months, the famed solar panels were permanently dead. The enclosure was installed on the main street in Mansfield, Ohio, on the town's busiest corner during working hours.

Ironically, it was dismantled and replaced by a normal pay phone enclosure in the middle of the night. What we announce during the day we remove under the cloak of darkness. That's how it works in PR…

CHAPTER

18

The Worst Coupon Ever To Appear In A Phone Directory

If you stay in public relations for any length of time, you will have to deal with a crisis. Many practitioners will tell you the key is to be prepared ahead of time, and then simply put your plan into action when the actual crisis arises.

As an example, I developed a crisis communications plan for a construction company client. Although no worker had ever been killed on a job site, we put it in the plan. A few months later a trench collapsed and an employee was killed. We were ready to deal with the situation.

But sometimes a company does something so unreal and so stupid that it is impossible to predict it. It happened to me in 1982.

My phone was ringing as soon as I came into the office in the morning. I was the spokesman for a local telephone company.

"John, we are in deep shit," said our Lima, Ohio, manager.

When somebody calls you at 8 a.m. and says you are in deep doo-doo, you know this is not going to be a good day. He then added, "Our new phone books are out."

Now, when you work at a phone company, when a new phone book comes out it is not exactly "breaking news." While we always hoped the media would greet it the way Steve Martin did in the movie "The Jerk" when he ran around yelling that he was now somebody because he was listed in the phone directory that does not happen often.

What does frequently happen is the new telephone directory lists the wrong phone number for the local police, ambulance service or some other vital service. We then issue stickers to all customers with the correct number. In other cases we give an advertiser a discount for having a wrong phone number in an ad, or some other thing to shut them up.

However, this sounded like something much worse. And it was.

"John, we've got a coupon in the phone book offering customers $25 off on an abortion," he said, with his voice cracking. "Geezus, we are screwed. We just delivered about 50,000 books and customers are going nuts!"

I honestly thought he was kidding. In fact, I did the "Gary, it is too damn early for this kind of a joke" response. Unfortunately, he wasn't kidding.

I quickly began gathering the facts. Yes, our famous directory couponing program, which our marketing folks had dubbed "one of the most innovative in the nation," certainly was breaking new ground, particularly in the area of abortions.

On top of the abortion coupon, there also was another one in the same directory offering a "Total Massage" and featured "XXX-Rated Videos." Actually, from a legal standpoint, the "Massage" coupon was really questionable; however, the abortion one drew all the attention.

The Worst Coupon Ever To Appear In A Phone Directory

Like a good sycophant, I took the news to our president and laid out the facts.

"Well, John, it certainly is going to attract lot of attention to our couponing program," he said with a grin. "Maybe we could charge other coupon advertisers extra for all the people who will be turning to the coupon section of the directory to see the abortion coupon."

Holy crap! I'm considering slitting my wrists and the president thinks it is kind of funny, I told him the people in Lima didn't share his sense of humor about the situation.

He then gave me that concerned, presidential look and said, "Handle the situation, John. Oh, and I'm not available for any interviews." Then he laughed again.

When something like this happens, the adrenaline starts to flow and a good PR person had damn well develop a plan of action—fast. I called the Lima people and asked a few questions:

- **How in the hell could an abortion coupon make it in the phone directory?** Well, we use an outside company to solicit ads and some clerk must have accepted it.

- **Are there ads we won't take?** Well, the rule has always been if you take out an ad, you can also buy a coupon. The abortion clinic had a Yellow Pages ad and…

- **How are customers reacting?** They are really pissed. We hired a guy to go and cut the coupons out of the directories at the Catholic hospital, but we can't get them out of every book in the area.

- **How is the media reacting?** At this point, they haven't contacted us yet, but it will hit the fan soon.

When you are in corporate public relations, there are times when you should handle an issue at the corporate level and times when it is better handled at the local level. Although one might say this was a local issue, I felt that this was going to be a major emotional issue and it would be better for me to take the heat.

Our Lima people had to live in the community and see their friends and neighbors every day. I would be some nameless, faceless corporate spokes-twit in another city who nobody in Lima knew They could hate me and then I could get the hell out of town.

It was time to check with the lawyers on all this. Corporate lawyers are like consultants—they can tell you 100 ways to have sex, but they can't get a date. They try to cover their butts by warning you to never do anything where anyone could ever sue you for any reason.

Their advice is generally so wishy-washy that it would cover abortion coupons, poor phone service and snake bites.

Here was the conversation about the coupons with our corporate legal guys:

- **Is the abortion coupon illegal?** No, not really. It really is more of an issue of tackiness. Since abortions are legal, a coupon offering a discount on one would be legal. Our policy is that if a customer takes out an ad in our phone directory, then he/she has an opportunity to have a coupon.

- **How about the "Total Massage" one?** We aren't sure, but it could be based on community standards in Lima.

- **Can I say we will never permit a coupon from an abortion clinic in the future in our directory?** Well, no. The woman who owns the abortion clinic has already threatened to sue us if we refuse to allow her to have future coupon ads.

- **How would you guys recommend I handle the media on this one?** Well, you could tell them that we did nothing illegal by offering the abortion coupon. Oh, and try to avoid talking about the massage one.

A trained monkey knew the public didn't want to hear a legal-smegal answer to an emotional issue. I always hate it when a company says "Nah-nah, we didn't do anything illegal" when they do something everyone knows is wrong and unethical. And just plain stupid.

At times like this, the corporate spokesperson must hear all points of view in the company—executive, legal, marketing, etc.

The Worst Coupon Ever To Appear In A Phone Directory

Then you do your own thing, since it is really your ass—your credibility—on the line.

My attitude was always to look long term. If you hide under your desk during a crisis, then don't go try to kiss the media's butt later on when you need something.

I drafted a statement of response for any incoming media inquiries. My statement was: **"Our company sincerely apologizes if we offended anyone with the coupon in the Lima telephone directory. We are taking steps now to insure that potentially controversial ads will not appear in future directories."**

From approximately 8:30 a.m. until nearly midnight, my phone rang nonstop. Some media people—particularly those farthest away from Lima—thought it was a hoot. One New York paper used it as a "Today's Chuckle" item.

Believe me, though, the people in Lima were not chuckling.

Whether you were pro-abortion, anti-abortion or didn't care one way or another, nearly everyone agreed having a coupon offering a $25 discount on one was tacky.

In Lima, the people were livid. The local Catholic school had a sign out front: "Abortion is a national disgrace, and so is United Telephone." Outraged customers were bombarding our switchboards to express their anger.

People marched outside our building. The poor Lima general manager, a good Irish Catholic, was getting it from all sides. He was actually pointed out during a church service as the GM for the phone company.

Our corporate executives—far away from the heat—thought the thing was a hoot. That was until other coupon advertisers threatened not to pay their bills because customers told them they were going to boycott their services.

I learned a big lesson that day—the vast majority of corporate executives care only about the bottom line. You can say their families will be shot and they won't blink an eye. Tell them their quarterly bonus may be impacted and you've got their attention.

I gave out the company statement well over 100 times the first day. People always bitch that the media are biased, and often they are. Hell, we are all biased. But to think the media is one big, unfeeling blob of mush is a little naive.

For 99 percent of them, they knew my balls were in a sling, and they appreciated that I would say *anything* about this monstrous screw-up. They appreciated that I would respond, even if it was corporate mush.

One of the worst calls I got involved being put on a talk radio show "live." By rights, radio shows are supposed to tell you they are recording your remarks. However, this guy put me on "live" without any warning and I was trapped by his irate callers for a half an hour. They really chewed my butt badly.

In due time (unfortunately, phone directories are around for a full year) the people of Lima went on to other things. No one ever asked about the massage coupon, and we dodged a bullet on that one.

CHAPTER

19

Other Crises: If You Want Sympathy, Die At Home

The CEO called me into his office and closed the door. Whenever he closed the door, it meant something bad was about to occur.

This executive was a bit strange. He was uber-rich and had an engineering degree from Yale, which always struck me as odd. The thought of him actually sitting at an engineering table and drawing specs for a men's restroom never entered my mind.

I went into his office one morning and he had his suit coat off. He was wearing an expensive white dress shirt with only the collar, cuffs and front nicely pressed. The rest of his shirt was so wrinkled it looked as if someone had taken a hammer to it. It was the strangest combination I had ever seen.

I later asked his secretary why his shirt looked like crap. She told me the CEO was in the process of getting a divorce and ironed his own shirts now. She said he ironed only those parts of the shirt people would notice when he wore a suit. I guess the thought of actually paying $1.50 to have it professionally cleaned and pressed was out of the question.

Being a Yalie, the CEO also had a huge sailboat. He would call me on a Friday afternoon and want me to recruit sailor-employees whenever he was going sailing. Luckily I had a list of sailor suckups who were willing to give up their weekend to be close to him and work like hell as his deck hands.

But I digress. I entered his office and he was smiling, barely able to hold back a chuckle.

"John, you aren't going to believe this," he said with a grin. "Jim (our VP of operations) was in a meeting at the parent company, went to take a piss, and died in the men's room. Can you believe it?"

Actually, I could believe Jim might die while pissing. He was horribly out of shape and a boozer. I just couldn't believe the CEO's humorous attitude about it, but that's corporate life. Jim's spot was filled within a week.

I had to put together a heartfelt message from our president about the passing of Jim to send to employees and the media. "He was a wonderful asset to our company and a dear friend to me," I wrote quoting the president.

A few years later, I was at a company where an executive came in smiling and happy in the morning. He then went out, bought a gun, came back to the office and blew his brains out. Again, the remaining executives pretended they cared, but most didn't.

Thank goodness he had the common decency to kill himself on a Friday. Within hours his office had been cleaned and recarpeted, and his replacement was ready to move in on Monday.

From a media standpoint, you develop a standard "We are shocked and upset that this unfortunate incident occurred" response. "He/she was a loyal and respected employee and will be sorely missed. Our prayers are with the family at this time of sorrow," or some such drivel.

However, first off you try to appeal to the media's sense of fairness and try to get them not to mention that a suicide occurred. Many people feel that a suicide that happens at work is work-related, and you certainly don't want to portray your company as Suicide Central. One reporter wrote, instead of suicide, that the executive "died suddenly at work." Yes, I believe it was "sudden."

True story: Our vice president of administration called us to the conference room. He announced that he had liver cancer and would be undergoing chemotherapy treatments. We were stunned because he was a really great guy. Our lobbyist broke the silence.

"Dick, a close friend of mine had liver cancer more than six years ago and is doing great today," he said. "They have wonderful treatments today."

We left the conference room and I told the lobbyist that it was great that his friend was doing so well with such a deadly disease.

"John, I just made that bullshit up," he said without batting an eye. "Dick will be dead in six months."

CHAPTER

20

Not All Short People Have A Napoleonic Complex

Yes, many executives and television folks do suffer from small-person's disease. They are short—or, in the vernacular of today, "vertically challenged"—and many spend their lives taking it out on the rest of the world.

However, the smallest person I have ever worked with was a dwarf sportswriter, and he was one of the most unique people I have ever met in my life. By nature, sportswriters are a strange breed. Most have been sports fanatics all their lives and never really grew up. That certainly summarized Dennis's life.

You have to love sports to listen to players say "You know" to start every sentence.

Well, anyway, Dennis absolutely loved sports. He would not only read everything that came across the news wires, but would take home reams of stories to read at night. He had one of those TV sets that got a million channels and he would watch sports stuff from around the world.

He was one of those characters who adds "color" to a sports department. I used to love to watch tours come through the department and see the looks on kids' faces when they'd see Dennis at his desk, unshaven, totally unkempt with his legs dangling about a foot off the floor. His desk always looked like it had been hand-grenaded.

There were only two things that Dennis hated: kids who thought he was a kid, and dogs. I felt sorry for the kids because he was probably the only dwarf they had ever met and many assumed he was just a kid with a beard. With dogs, I would have hated them, too, if I'd had to look at them eye-to-eye.

I used to feel sorry for tour groups going through our Sports Department. It was in the days when everyone smoked and the place smelled like a three-day-old fart. It also was during the time when everyone had real typewriters and yelled back and forth over the clanging keys.

My main contribution for tours was an ability to take rubber cement, roll it into shape and put it up my nose. When the tour would come by I would casually pull out his huge rubber cement "booger." The guys loved it. The tour people were disgusted.

Dennis could get away with doing some of the damnedest things. If the desk editor asked him for two pages on a sports item, he would write four. He always "wrote long," which irritates the hell out of editors.

One time he turned in a story 12 pages long when they asked for two. In those days, all the pages were pasted to each other, and his 12-pager was about 10 feet in length. One of the editors looked at it, held it up and cut off everything from page two on.

When this happened, Dennis would run over and try to argue the merits of his story. Because of his size he would be eye to eye with the editors while they were sitting. Then he would grab their shirt and tug on it while making his point. That would really piss them off. There would be a million things going on and Dennis would be tugging on an editor's arm.

One time an editor warned Dennis not to come over and harass him about a story.

Dennis still nagged him and nagged him. We watched the smoke start to come from the editor's ears. I told my co-workers, "If Dennis grabs his arm, I think the editor will kill him."

No sooner had I said that than Dennis started tugging on his shirt to make a point. Without blinking an eye, the editor reached over, pulled his brush out of the paste container, stuck it right in Dennis's mouth and mushed it around. Dennis got a mouthful of paste and ran around spitting the stuff out of his mouth. He didn't bother that editor for almost two whole days.

Another time Dennis drove a copy editor to the point where he grabbed him and put him in one of those large garbage containers—head first. Still another time, one of the guys picked Dennis up and put him on top of the file cabinets. He might as well have been on Mount Everest. He begged me to bring him down and I relented, but I almost peed on myself from laughing so hard.

One of Dennis's most endearing traits—in addition to writing long—was that he didn't write very well. His stories often ended up looking good in the paper, but they were often heavily edited. We would kid him about his writing, but he would just laugh and write some more.

One time the sports editor ordered copies of Strunk and White's famous book "The Elements of Style" for everyone in the department. This gesture was really directed at Dennis, but the editor felt it best to chastise all of us.

Dennis picked up his unread copy, laughed, autographed it and gave it to me as a gift. I left the sportswriting club a short while later, and a few years later Dennis went to the great sports department in the sky. However, I still treasure that book.

CHAPTER
21

Off Our Rockers Over Walter Cronkite

I would say that working with the late legendary broadcasting icon Walter Cronkite gave me the biggest thrill of my PR life. What a class act.

A hospital I was working with was celebrating its anniversary and Walter was to be the guest speaker. Walter had numerous ties to the Kansas City area and had agreed to help us out.

One of the things Walter had agreed to do was visit the hospital's Infant Development Center, where he would meet these special-needs children and spend some time with them. It was his

80th birthday and he was to sit in a rocking chair as the kids sang "Happy Birthday" to him and bring out a cake.

On the day of his visit I suggested we should do a run-through prior to his arrival. Of course, most people thought it was a pain, but I didn't care. Actually, it gave me a chance to do my awful impersonation of Walter.

I walked in slowly (it was his 80th birthday, after all) and did my "And that's the way it is, November 2, 1954" Walter Cronkite voice. For you youngsters, that was the way he signed off his broadcasts.

I then went over and sat in the special rocking chair in place for Walter. The only problem was the chair seemed way too low on the floor. It immediately dawned on me that Walter was going to have a heckuva time getting out of the damn thing.

And then I noticed something else. The rocking chair didn't rock. This was not a good sign.

I looked down and realized the maintenance guy who had assembled the rocking chair had forgotten to put the rocker things on the bottom of the legs! He had simply taken the new chair out of the box and plopped it down.

Holy crap! Someone ran out to the dumpster and found the chair's packing box and retrieved the rockers that go on the bottom of the chair. An executive used a coin to screw them in just minutes before Walter arrived.

And that's why it is important for PR folks to follow the Boy Scout motto of "Be Prepared." You can never tell when your rocking chair will not rock…

CHAPTER

22

We Have The Situation Completely Under Control—Almost

The wonderful people of Lima, Ohio, not only had the opportunity to have the world's first and only discount coupon for abortions, but they also had one of the largest telephone outages ever.

One of our executives called me and said we had another "problem" in Lima. It seems as if our local switch was out of service and Lima customers could not make or receive any calls. It had been down a few hours, but we anticipated it being back in service "any minute now."

This was a case (again) where it was felt that "corporate" communications could handle the situation and then leave town. Our local people could then save face and tell their friends that this was all a corporate screw-up. I was used to playing the role of the corporate guy.

When we arrived, the phone service had been down for about six hours—which is a hell of a long time for an entire city to be without any phone service. Our crack engineers had absolutely no idea what was causing the outage. Heck, for all I knew, there were gerbils operating the switch.

Keep in mind, this was when the "DFC," Duh Telephone Company, handled all the phone calls in an area. There were no such things as cell phones in those days.

We had telephone trucks at major intersections equipped with radio transmitters. If you had to make a call in an emergency, you could go to the truck and they could possibly relay it through, but otherwise, everything stopped in Lima that day.

From a media standpoint, it was a mess. Most media people from Columbus and other areas simply drove or flew in helicopters and planes to Lima for the story. I had media people standing in line outside a room and they came in one-by-one for interviews with me. I'd do a TV interview, then a radio, then a print, then another TV, etc.

During each interview I'd say that we hope to have the switch completely operational "at any time." I always added that we would like to especially thank the "wonderful people of Lima for their patience and support during this outage."

The hours dragged on. Our engineers were so dumbfounded over the problem that I was beginning to think my gerbil story might be valid. My biggest worry was that some bad people might decide to rob all of Lima and we'd be responsible.

Well, 19 hours later the switch was up and running. Actually, it was up in 18 hours, but when people learned they now had phone service, they all tried to call at the same time. This crush of calls caused the damn switch to crash again. At 19 hours it went on again and all was well.

The people of Lima were really terrific during the outage. I guess after an abortion coupon you learn to deal with all kinds of ordeals with the phone company. Best of all, they paid us in full for nearly a full day without service. Our executives were ecstatic.

CHAPTER

23

When The Media Screws Up

As a PR person, sometimes you can do everything perfectly and things can still turn to crap.

More often than not you can feel you media-trained someone magnificently only to have him/her blurt out something or do something that is just plain stupid.

As an example, I spent hours with the founder of a company briefing him for a business interview. My main concern was that he might blurt out some politically incorrect response, which he was known to do—on a daily basis.

His views on women, blacks, Hispanics, etc., were from another generation—likely around the 1870s. If the term "politically incorrect" had been in the dictionary at the time, it would have had a picture of him.

When the female reporter came into his office, he immediately ignored all my training and said, "Welcome to my company, honey." He then walked over to her and gave her a big kiss.

I was stunned, but he wasn't finished. He then proceeded to light up a cigarette and say, "Is it okay to smoke, honey?" to the dumbfounded reporter.

Luckily the reporter was sympathetic to the situation because the owner was about 80-years-old and reminded her of her own politically incorrect grandfather. Whew.

But sometimes the media screw up and the PR person is left to pick up the pieces. As an example, a TV crew came to my engineering company to do a 20-minute piece about the guys who build our models (see earlier chapter).

Trust me, a TV crew in your office for most of a day is a major pain in the butt. They disrupt everything and I was constantly telling employees if they don't want to be in the shot to disappear. Workplace productivity that day was probably around 5 percent.

When the piece finally aired it was superb. Except for the part where they completely forgot to mention *the name of our damn company!* Yes, they somehow forgot to mention exactly where they were.

To this day the screw-up amazes me. When I told the producer about it, he told me that was impossible. I told him to sit down and watch the damn segment. His apology didn't make me feel much better.

One of my favorite media screw-ups actually worked in my favor. A reporter from a small paper came to do a story about a company I was representing. It was called "ChoicePoint" and he spent about half a day interviewing executive staffers.

We eagerly awaited his feature story to come out. However, somewhere along the line the reporter thought the name of the company was "CheckPoint." It was likely just some sort of reporter brain fart, but my client was livid. When the name of his company was wrong in the newspaper

"Call the x&%$) editor and tell him I want a x&)@### correction," said my incensed client. There is mad, and then there is very mad. My client was very, very mad.

Most PR folks would have immediately called the paper's editor and demanded a correction. The reporter would have been in major trouble, or even fired.

But, as they say, that's not how I roll.

I called the reporter and joked I could get him to say "Oh, crap!" Then I told him about the name screw-up in the newspaper and he replied, "Oh, crap!" (Okay, that wasn't the exact word he said, but you get the point.)

The reporter was devastated. He said he would do a correction (that would likely be buried on page E-12 in the paper) saying, "The name of the company we featured should have been 'ChoicePoint.'"

My solution? I told the reporter, let's keep this screw-up between us kids. First, just fix the name in the story and then we can get corrected reprints and still use them in our marketing efforts.

Then, a few months down the road he agreed he would come back and do another feature on the company highlighting another aspect of it. There was no need for his editor to ever know about the error, and it would be a win-win for everyone.

He thought it was a wonderful idea and thanked me profusely for not going to his editor to complain.

"You used to work at a newspaper, didn't you?" he asked.

"Yes," I said. "And I hated when people complained to my editor and got me in trouble."

CHAPTER

24

The Shame Of It All! Sucking Up To Influencers

Recently, The Associated Press reported that the "former Countrywide Financial Corp., whose subprime loans helped start the nation's foreclosure crisis, made hundreds of discount loans to buy influence with members of Congress, congressional staff, top government officials and executives of troubled mortgage giant Fannie Mae," according to a House report.

"The report, obtained by The Associated Press, said the discounts were not only aimed at gaining influence for the company but to help mortgage giant Fannie Mae."

At least one reporter at NPR acted shocked at the revelation that such favoritism could occur.

To me, the story could have then gone on with "And in other news, water is wet and the sun will be rising in the east...."

In reality, companies having special lists of "influencers" is a common tactic in public relations circles. In fact, in many cases it is an accepted business practice that has been in effect for decades.

The reality is that all customers are not created equal. Someone buying your product once a year is not nearly as valuable as someone who buys it each week. That is life. Deal with it.

Business people also know there are "normal" customers and then there are people who are considered "influencers." There is a huge difference.

Influencers are the ones who can make critical decisions that can impact your business—positively or negatively. Their decisions influence others' decisions. They might be elected officials, media folks, prominent business owners, etc.

As an example, luxury car manufacturers know that if the "right" people drive their cars, it will influence others to buy them. The president of our company drove a top-of-the-line Cadillac. Why? Because he was identified by General Motors as an "influencer," and GM gave huge discounts to corporate executives just so they would be seen driving around the community in their cars.

Ironically, while the media have jumped all over Countrywide for its program of giving loans to members of Congress and government staffers, many of these programs often include members of the media. Mine always did.

To be honest, some media influencers are not even aware that they are on a company's "special" customer list. The best programs are often the most subtle ones.

We had one beat writer who was a total deadbeat. His bills were often not paid within 90 days (if at all). If he were a normal customer we would have either shut off his service or sent his account to a collection agency.

He was on our special "influencer" list. How could he complain about our company? Heck, we kissed his butt so much that he would be hard-pressed to write something negative about us.

When dealing with the media you cannot ever reveal to them that they might be on a "special" list. They would be offended, particularly print reporters. They feel they are just "regular" folk.

The reality is that the news media are one of the most powerful forces in nature today. Many of them are considered "influencers" on company lists across the country. If they aren't on your list, they should be.

CHAPTER
25

"I Have A Collect Call From A Convict…"

One of the most unique cons I ever dealt with involved women accepting collect calls. The callers, all men, would then tell these women that their husbands had been kidnapped and they must send a ransom or their husbands would be harmed.

While it is doubtful many of these women actually sent money, it certainly scared the hell out of many of them. I'm sure some sent the money.

There were a rash of these calls over period of a couple weeks. We traced the calls back to a prison in another state. The callers were honest-to-goodness convicts and this was recreation for them. It sure made me feel good about the penal system when nimrods like these guys could try to extort money as part of their rehabilitation.

The media called, and their main question was "Why would people accept a collect call from a criminal?" My answer was that many people answering the phone don't actually hear the person's name, but assume it must be someone they know who needs help. I felt sorry for these women and I wasn't going to put them down.

I did, however, say that "In the future, we sincerely hope the Michigan prison system develops new forms of recreation for their inmates." While I am a notorious smart-ass, most of my media responses are pretty straight.

In this case, though, I figured taking a pot shot at a prison system in another state was safe. I grew up in Ohio and we don't like Michigan folks anyway.

CHAPTER

26

Please, Lord, Not A Groundbreaking!

Rumors had persisted for months that our company was considering expanding and was going to need a new headquarters building.

No problem. It's a good story about growth and what the growth will mean to the community. I would pitch that story to the media every day of my life.

We made the announcement and it was a media hit. We had those nice architectural drawings of the new building complete with lovely landscaping. All was good.

Then I was told the president was looking forward to some great coverage of a planned groundbreaking. My first thought was to find a window on the 10th floor and jump the hell out.

Groundbreakings are PR nightmares. Just the thought of a bunch of corporate folks standing there with gold shovels pretending to use them is beyond frightening to a PR flack.

You can try all kinds of unique ways to do a groundbreaking, but they all pretty much suck. A PR guy in Cleveland once thought it would be cool for the mayor to use a blowtorch and "cut" some sort of metal ribbon at his groundbreaking. Unfortunately, the torch was facing the mayor, and the front page of almost every newspaper in the nation showed the mayor with his hair on fire.

Our groundbreaking was scheduled. It was going to be 12 idiots with shovels. I began calling the media inviting them to this event. It was awful.

"Hey, Bill, I wanted to invite you to our groundbreaking next week," I said.

"We have a company policy of not covering any groundbreakings," he replied.

"Bill, we will have some nice food and giveaway items. It will only take about a half-hour," I said as my voice gradually went from conversational to groveling.

"John, I actually will get in trouble even asking my editor to cover a groundbreaking," he said. "We hate those damn things."

After numerous calls, *every* damn media person turned me down. The radio guy scoffed that shovels going into the ground did not make for compelling radio.

"Bill, this is John again," I said in full grovel mode. "You have to come to the groundbreaking. I will do anything to get your butt here. I'll have sex with you, your wife and dog. I'll paint your house. Please, I am beyond begging…."

"John, while it would be nice to have sex with you, I will get fired if I even go to the groundbreaking. I just can't do it."

I had completely struck out. I decided to crawl into my boss's office and admit that not one damn media person was interested in our groundbreaking.

"I am dead in the water," I said. "We are going to have a groundbreaking with no media people there. I am screwed."

My boss laughed. It often seems that when I am serious, other folks break into laughter.

"I heard you on the phone offering sex to the print reporter," he said, trying to hold back tears from guffawing so much. "I had never heard a PR guy offer to have sex with a reporter's dog if he would come to an event."

"Okay, maybe I went overboard…a bit," I said, "but what can we do?"

"It's really pretty simple. Just go out and hire four or five folks and have them shoot video and take lots of pictures and pretend they are with the news media," he said matter-of-factly.

"Our executives just want their pictures taken a lot. We can tell them that our groundbreaking story was bumped from the media outlets at the last moment. They will never know," he added.

And that is why he was my boss. Our paid fake media people took miles of video and shot photo after photo. Our president was happy as a lark at the "great media coverage."

And I was hoping to never have to publicize a groundbreaking again in my life.

CHAPTER

27

The Annual Report Cover From Hell

If you ever have an opportunity to write an annual report, I have some sage advice: Avoid it at all costs.

As a PR person, your job is to write all the happy news in the front section and then let the bean counters do all the financial stuff. Sometimes the two sides can be completely different.

The PR person also often picks the printer and photos and determines the cover. Keep in mind, most businesses act as if the annual report is second only to the Ten Commandments in importance. That means a typo can be career shortening.

When it comes to annual reports, everything has to be approved by nearly everyone at the damn corporation. And there are very strict rules about exactly when it has to be printed and distributed. If not done correctly, heads definitely will roll, and it is often your head that will be the first to go.

Having done seven annual reports in my career, I know the process. It is awful. You write the first draft and send it for approval. Change upon change keeps rolling in. Everyone feels he/she needs to put his/her particular stamp on it.

The process can go on for weeks. About halfway through it, any pride of authorship is gone. About three-fourths of the way through, you simply don't give a crap about it and just want the process to end. You make changes to copy that had been changed already five times.

One annual report was a classic that I will never forget—no matter how hard I try. Everything was approved. All the verbiage, all the photos, the paper stock, the cover, the typestyle, etc. I gave the go-ahead to the printer to begin printing literally thousands of copies with a beautiful black, glossy cover.

Even the printing of annual reports takes days. They have to be printed and the ink has to dry. When done, you grab the first copy and hand-deliver it to the president.

My boss was the one honored to take the first copy of the report to our president. He came into my office looking dejected.

"The president wants more blue in the cover," reported my boss.

"Holy crap!" I shouted. "We can't reprint thousands of annual reports before tomorrow's deadline. He signed off on the cover. We are screwed."

My boss had been through this kind of thing before and never was rattled. As they say, this was not his first rodeo.

"I'll take care of it," he said with a slight grin. Again, when I am serious people seem to laugh the hardest.

"How exactly are you going to add blue to the damn cover after it has been printed?" I said, totally beside myself.

"I'm not. I'm going to wait until this afternoon and take the same annual report back down to him and tell him we added just a touch of blue to the cover," he said. "If I tell him blue was added, he will think he sees some blue and we'll be home free."

I was stunned. It was one of the ballsiest tricks I had ever heard of in my corporate life.

Sure enough. My boss took the same annual report to the president and pretended that we had somehow added blue to it as he wanted. The president loved it.

I am still in awe that my boss was able to pull off that trick. It was a corporate work of art.

CHAPTER

28

"Leaving To Pursue Other Interests": His Butt Has Been Canned

"Mr. Snotass has left the company to pursue other interests." In PR code: "He was fired."
Same for the "He resigned to spend more time with his family" reason. Let's face it, most executives are such workaholics they might not be able to tell you're their kids' names off the top of their head.

For the most part, journalists expect this kind of drivel when an executive leaves. We stole one top executive from a company and ballyhooed it like we had recruited God to our company. After working with him a year, people referred to him as "a true genius," a "man of vision" and "one of the most knowledgeable in the industry." I personally thought he was a jerk, but he dealt with technical things, so what did I know.

When he announced he was leaving to join our major competitor, you would have thought he had leprosy. In one day's time, he had gone from "genius" and "visionary" to "disloyal," unethical," "money-grubbing," etc.

At one point our executives wanted to do a slam-dunk on this guy and announce we were going to sue his butt, burn his house down, kill his family and the like. However, they decided against it.

The executive rule when another executive leaves for questionable reasons is to not say anything bad externally about him. This is basically because most of the executives have a "There but for the grace of God go I" kind of attitude. They know they would screw the company in a New York minute if given the opportunity.

I have been involved in communicating layoffs at a number of companies. From my standpoint, I hate it and would just as soon never have to do it again. Part of my consideration comes from seeing layoffs from a number of views:

> **Executives**—To most of them, letting nameless, faceless people go bothers them as much as a hangnail. In most cases, it is strictly a numbers thing where the accountants say "margins are down" and to get margins up people must go. Remember, higher margins mean higher bonuses.
>
> **Analysts**—They love layoffs because it means the company is "streamlining" or making these moves to "increase margins." The more heads roll, the happier the analysts are.
>
> **Consultants**—They love layoffs because companies lay people off and they can come in and do "consulting."

"Leaving To Pursue Other Interests": His Butt Has Been Canned

Employees—Layoffs are real bummers to employees. If your name is on the list, it means a steady stream of Jerry Springer, Dr. Oz, Dr. Phil and the gang on daytime TV.

One company where I worked had a series of quarters of record earnings and profits. Each time, we held "thank you" events for employees because "We Care" and "Employees are Our Greatest Asset."

Then, we laid off several hundred employees because we wanted to take action "from a position of strength," according to our president. Boy, did that send a strange message to the employees: "Gee, if I work hard and the company is profitable, I get laid off because they wanted to do it from a position of strength."

That sure would be an interesting topic for a Junior Achievement class for kids on how business operates.

CHAPTER

29

The One Word That Causes Executive Urination

There are few things that will cause normally mild-mannered executives to become absolute lunatics. Next to telling them that their bonus is being eliminated, mention the word "union" and watch them wet their Hickey Freeman suits.

I've worked at totally union companies, totally non-union companies and a couple of in-betweens. In union shops all bad things happen because of unions. If a toilet overflows, it is a union trick.

If it snows heavily and workers have a tough time making it in on time, the damn union was behind it.

Actually, in most cases, I often felt that without unions it would take most executives about a decade before they'd have 6-year-olds (not their own kids, mind you) working 14-hour shifts for $1.25 per hour. And, when they were a week from retirement, they'd can them.

In non-union companies executives go ballistic at the very first mention of "organizing." In many ways it's kind of funny since most unions are so disorganized that they couldn't organize a neighborhood party.

As an example, unions attempting to organize a company where I worked sent out a news release saying pretty much how our company gouged out employees' eyes, took bullwhips to them daily and molested their children. This would be quite a dramatic piece of information; however, union news releases frequently have so many misspellings, typos and grammatical mistakes common to three-year-olds that reporters would laugh when they received them.

From the company's standpoint, we always would issue a basic "We do not respond to allegations brought up by union organizers. Our employees have chosen not to be represented by the union and we respect their wishes." In the meantime, we would hold "Employee Appreciation Days" and the like until the union threat blew over.

Where the union really blows it is in the media relations arena. When a newspaper or radio station tries to find a union spokesperson, it is next to impossible. One newspaper guy said he tried numerous times to get anyone from the union to speak to him about charges made in a news release.

"Finally, I contacted the union's national headquarters in Washington for a statement," said the reporter. "They had a recording that said, 'We ain't available today due to having Columbia (Columbus) Day off. Call us back in the morning.'" Needless to say, the reporter never made contact with the union folks.

Union folks attending a company's annual meeting are often about as discreet as turds in a punchbowl. While everyone else is nattily dressed in their very best business outfits, the union folks generally are adorned in black silk jackets that are emblazoned with "Local 1022, Workers of the World."

They sit together, and when it is question time, they say things like: "Yeah, I'm Bill Jones from Local 1022 of Workers of the World. I wanna know why youse make your workers come in on time and work a full eight-hour day. If they was in a union they would only have to work four hours a day and make twice as much money."

And unions wonder why their ranks are declining…

CHAPTER

30

Let's Hold A Meeting, I Didn't Have Anything Better To Do

In business, 98 percent of all meetings are a waste of time. This is an exact percent that I have learned from more than 25 years of attending, directing and participating in meetings. However, since many businesses exist to hold meetings, they are an integral part of our culture.

In local meetings, people come together for a common purpose: to do their level best to avoid any potential tasks that might involve work. Otherwise, meetings are good for chatting about upcoming football games, corporate gossip, TV programs and other generic topics.

There are certain important keys about meetings:

- Avoid any meetings that start before normal working hours or any that are scheduled to go past normal closing time. These meetings are being held by bona fide corporate sycophants who are trying to impress someone higher up.
- Any person who holds a meeting on a weekend is not only a sycophant, but also one that doesn't have a life. Avoid these meetings at all costs.
- Always act like the meeting you are attending is on the same level of whether a nuclear war is necessary, and act genuinely interested. If you can walk out of the meeting without a specific task, you have accomplished a major goal.

The only thing more wasteful than a normal business meeting is one where travel is involved. A wise co-worker early on in my career gave me some wonderful advice prior to a meeting.

"If there are 30 things on the agenda to be accomplished, the first five items will be debated for hours; the next 10 will be approved in about five minutes, and the remaining 15 will be on hold for a future meeting," he said with a chuckle. He was right on target.

I saw it in action at our next meeting. People flew in from all over the country and we stayed at a lavish hotel. Although the meeting was supposed to start at 8 a.m. on Wednesday morning and conclude Thursday at 5 p.m., some attendees arrived as early as 9 a.m. Tuesday "to handle other issues."

These "other" issues included shopping, visiting relatives and swimming. Oh, and drinking. Serious drinking.

The meeting went exactly as my co-worker predicted. We debated the first item on the agenda for two hours. The second item was discussed until lunch. The afternoon saw us tackle three more before adjourning for dinner.

The next day—and I swear this has happened in every out-of-town meeting I have ever attended—the meeting leader says something like, "Well, I think we accomplished a lot yesterday, but we still have 25 more issues to address before the meeting ends this afternoon, so I would recommend we get started and try to get through them as quickly as possible."

At that point, at least one attendee says, "By the way, Bill I had to book an early flight back home and it leaves in about three hours." Then, other attendees start to chime in their flight times. "My flight's at noon." "Yeah, I could only get out on the two o'clock flight."

The meeting leader then gets an exasperated look and says, "Well, we had better get moving." Then, topics get approved in supersonic time with little discussion as everyone approves everything.

If an item you care about falls into this time frame, you are home free: "I think that we should move the company into a three-day workweek and double everyone's salary. Any discussion? No? Great, let's move on to the next item."

Around 2 p.m. on Thursday people are slipping out of the meeting like rats deserting a sinking ship. The meeting has officially slipped into a weird state of confusion where nobody can keep track of the discussion with people grabbing bags, trying to get rides to the airport, discussing frequent flyer points, etc.

By 3 p.m. the meeting officially concludes with the remaining people agreeing that another meeting is necessary to handle the final 15 agenda items.

"How does everyone feel about getting together in Florida in December to go over the remaining items?" says the meeting leader. "I'll send a memo to you on it."

CHAPTER

31

The Company's Designated "Pin Pimp"

A lot of folks see the PR person on TV or quoted in the paper saying wonderful things about the company. And it is fun doing that—as long as the news is positive.

But, sometimes, as you may have guessed so far in this book, PR people have other duties that are not quite as glamorous as a TV appearance.

One day my CEO called me in and said it would be nice if our employees showed their pride in the company. And he knew a great way for them to show it.

He had just met with a promotional items vendor (cute, very cute) and she said if all employees would wear a company logo pin, it would show their pride in our company.

He thought it was a great idea and had already ordered thousands of the pins. About 40,000 of them.

Of course, I told him I thought the pin idea was one of the greatest ideas mankind had ever seen. To me, every new CEO idea was hard to top.

We had thousands of pins produced and we gave one to every employee. We let the employees know this was the CEO's idea, and, in a very nice way, let them know if the CEO saw them not wearing the pin, they were in big trouble. We never liked to actually threaten employees since it was bad for morale.

I swear, within hours friends were calling to say they lost their pin or their pin broke. Women complained that the pins poked holes in their blouses. I could see that a simple damn pin program was getting out of hand very quickly.

I received a call from a vice president's secretary.

"John, I understand you are the company's pin pimp," she said trying to suppress an all-out laugh. "My VP needs six more pins."

"Why exactly would he need more pins already?" I said, knowing the title "Pin Pimp" was already bestowed on me.

"He said he needs one for every suit he has," she noted. "You don't actually think he would be able to take a pin off one suit and put it on another."

So I gave her six more pins. Word spread among the executive staff that they should have pins for every suit and that her VP had six. I was delivering pins all along executive row. They were like pigs in poo. They couldn't get enough pins.

The program was a complete pain in the butt. I walked around with my suit pockets filled with pins. Every time I saw an executive without a pin I would discreetly go over to him like some sort of drug pusher and slip him a pin to put on. Friends who found themselves without their pin heading into an executive meeting would hit me up for one.

I learned to hate the damn pins. The program lasted about six months. I knew it was going to end after an executive took me aside and had a special request.

"John, I think the pins look kind of cheap," he said. "I think that it would be nice if executive staffers had nice gold ones."

Yes, when all was said and done, the executives really were upset that they were stuck wearing gold-colored metal pins that were the same as the lowly employees. Yes, I ordered expensive real gold pins for the executive staffers, but as the word spread of the "special" pins, the program kind of faded away. I didn't miss it.

CHAPTER

32

Human Resources: Why Idiots Get Hired

If you are a normal person trying to get a job, then you have had to deal with Human Resources people. Next to Public Relations, the Human Resources Department is the biggest dumping ground for incompetents in a company. Unfortunately, you must get by HR people if you hope for employment.

If a new governmental guideline comes out saying that "All companies with more than five employees must have at least one black midget of Ethiopian heritage who is a Vietnam veteran," then either HR or PR will get one.

HR will get one for Equal Employment Opportunity Commission reasons, or PR will get one for publicity purposes to show the world how our wonderful company "celebrates diversity."

At one point in my career I was attached to the HR Department. It was fascinating to actually talk with these people as a trusted accomplice. It can also be quite discouraging.

If you are a black woman and don't get a job you are eminently qualified for, you very well could think it was because of your race. However, it could be because the HR person interviewing you didn't like your purse. Or maybe the HR person didn't like the mole on your face.

"I never hire anyone with red hair," boasted one VP of HR I worked with. "They are too hot-headed and cause problems. I've never hired one in 20 years."

Anyone else? "Yeah, I wouldn't even consider hiring someone who smoked a pipe," he added with that look of a person who is just about the smartest sonofabitch in the world. "Pipe smokers analyze things too much. By the time they ponder everything and start to make a decision, the issue has passed. I've never hired one."

It sure made me feel good that this wasn't a race thing, but rather personal hang-ups. We dummies come in all dressed up, say the right things, think the interview has gone extremely well and then get the dreaded "Thank you for your interest in National Toilet Company..." because the HR dweeb thinks you might smoke a pipe.

Until my conversations with HR people, I used to take job rejections personally. Now, I realize there are factors I have no control over that cause people not to get a job, the least of which might be qualifications.

I have lost a job because I wasn't Jewish, but the one I lost because I was Catholic was a classic. I was contacted by the PR guy for a major steel company in Pittsburgh about a position in Cleveland. I had lunch with him, then, a week later, with his assistant. Both went very well.

They then asked me to come to Pittsburgh for full day of psychological testing to see if I was suited for a PR position with their company. Seeing as I had been in PR for nearly 10 years, I had hoped that I was suited for it. As luck would have it, I passed the test and was ready to meet the Cleveland Division president.

During the interview the president was very cordial and seemed like a competent guy. I did notice that he mentioned God a few times when talking about employees and steel production. This struck me as odd since I didn't know there was any kind of relationship between the two.

As the interview was wrapping up, the president looked at me sincerely and said, "John, what religion are you?"

Panic set in. An internal alarm immediately went off in my body that said, "This sonofabitch isn't allowed to ask me that."

Of course, if I actually told him that he wasn't allowed to ask me that question, he would have half-apologized. I then would have landed the job just about the same time hell froze over.

Then, my mind flashed back to the nuns who always talked about saints who gave their lives rather than deny their religion. Of course, I should have stood up and said proudly, "Catholic!"

In reality, I said meekly, "Catholic?" in a voice that really said, "Did I guess correctly?"

He gave me that half smile that said, "I'll pretend that your answer didn't eliminate you from this position, but in reality I wouldn't hire a Catholic in a million years." I knew I was dead.

The PR guy was waiting outside for me. "How did it go, John?" he asked enthusiastically. I said it went very well up until the president asked me about my religion.

"He asked you what religion you are?" he said. "What did you tell him?"

I said, "Catholic."

"You're dead," he said, sadly

If you are looking for a job, keep in mind that over time these things balance out. The steel company is now history. However, I later landed a job with a large company because they thought I was Jewish. Did you know there are a lot of Jewish Rabbis named Landsberg?

I adapted. I learned about Jewish holidays and took them off just like the Jewish employees did. It was great! I learned that Jewish people not only get Christmas and other holidays off, but also their own religious holidays.

I told them the truth after my going-away party…oy vey!

CHAPTER

33

The Bobby Knight News Conference

Corporations love to have big meetings and love to invite sports people to address them. There is a feeling that a famous player or coach can impart some nuggets of knowledge that will motivate employees to greatness.

Jocks who can put two sentences together without stumbling can receive literally thousands of dollars for these gigs. A friend told me his company used to have Mickey Mantle give talks about his career. Mick was so drunk at one appearance, he fell over in the middle of the speech, got back up and continued talking. My friend said it looked like Mick had done that before.

I have found having most jocks give talks is silly, but what the hell. After two days of intense meetings about corporate goals, sales projections and the like, having a jock come and say stupid things can be fun.

Things like "We is all one big team. We is unique, you know. I remember this guy, you know, who hit me so hard that snot bubbles came out of my nose. But I didn't quit. On the next play I gave him a forearm to his testicles that ended his sex life." At this point the audience cheers.

Several years ago our annual sales meeting was being organized. During the planning meeting, the top executives asked if anyone had any ideas which sports celebrity they could get to come speak to us.

One staffer, in an effort to get his nose a little browner, volunteered that he and Bobby Knight, the famous Indiana basketball coach, were high school classmates. This sycophant said Knight's mother lived nearby and he was sure if we agreed to pay for his trip home he'd speak to our group for free.

It was unanimous: Let's get Bobby Knight. Bobby Knight, he of the famous temper. Bobby Knight, the one who threw a chair across the basketball court in a rage. Bobby Knight, the one who could give a look that caused players to lose control of their bodily functions.

I called the guy who agreed to get Knight to speak and told him I was going to schedule a news conference for Knight.

"Hell, Bobby hates the media," he said.

I told him that if the media found out we were bringing Bobby Knight to our small town and didn't let them know, they would hate our company forever. He reluctantly agreed to tell Knight about the news conference—while he was en route to the speech.

Yes, this was Bobby Knight—notorious media hater—who once said disdainfully to the media, "All of us learn to write by the second grade, then most of us go on to other things." It is really ironic that today Knight is part of the media he hated so much.

Knight arrived at the hotel and looked irritated that he was scheduled for a press conference. When Knight looks irritated, he looks irritated. I gently ushered him into a small room and about 10 media people were in attendance. It was the first time I have ever seen the media totally intimidated.

"What brings you into our town, Mr. Knight," said one trembling reporter.

"I'm giving a speech to these folks," Knight said in a tone that led you to believe he didn't know if these "folks" sold phones, enema medicine or nuclear bombs. Or that he cared one way or another.

"Are you here on a recruiting mission?"

"No."

"Are you aware of Joe Blow (a local high school star who was idolized in the community and considered locally as a future professional prospect)?"

"I'm aware of him," said Knight. "He's too slow." The media people were crushed that the local hero had been dismissed so unceremoniously.

At that point Knight gave the assembled media "the look." The silence was deafening. The media people wanted to be anywhere but in a room with Bobby Knight. So did I.

"Oh, before I leave, I'd like to give you guys a scoop," said Knight as the media folks' ears popped up. "I'm opening up a furniture store in Indiana."

The media people were scribbling furiously at this hot news item.

"Yeah, our slogan is going to be 'If you buy a couch, Bobby Knight will throw in a chair.' " Knight roared in laughter. The assembled media didn't think it was that funny.

Knight later spoke to our group and did a great job of telling "inside" stories that he probably has told no less than a thousand times to hundreds of groups. The audience loved him despite his dropping f-bombs throughout his talk.

He later sent his friend a significant bill for his "free talk." We looked on it as his fee was spread out over 400,000 telephone customers. They probably didn't even notice.

CHAPTER

34

The Only Place Where The Truth Is Told: The Men's Restroom

Lying is an art form at corporations. People who can look at you sincerely and lie are destined for greatness. One executive told me, "Once you rise to the level of president of a company, nobody tells you the truth." He was absolutely on target.

There is only one area of a company where total honesty prevails—the men's restroom. If a company really wants to know what is going on in an organization, they should bug the restrooms.

Okay, I don't recommend using video—that would be sick and perverted—just a couple of microphones in strategic places above the urinals. Sure, it might violate some sort of privacy laws, but what the heck, that's why corporations have lawyers.

Thousands of times each day people sit in meetings and rave about how super a new product or service is. Then they go into the restroom and say how stupid the whole idea is and why it won't work.

This is a true example: An executive was addressing our group about how the quality process "will revolutionize the way we do business. Quality will permeate everything we do and say as we go forward and will be the linchpin of our future success."

At this point one of the attendees raised his hand and said, "I wholeheartedly agree with you, sir. Quality does represent the future of our company and—speaking for myself—I am glad that you have the vision and the foresight to lead us down the quality path."

The rest of the group cheered. The executive smiled broadly. You can tell he knew his audience "got" his message.

At the break we headed to the restroom. After a quick scan of the stalls, the employee who had just lavishly complimented the executive said, "How's that for blowing smoke up his ass?" and he laughed uproariously.

"That dumb sucker couldn't lead his finger out of his ass, much less a quality program."

"Geez, Fred, you had that moron believing that crap you were saying," added another guy.

"Fred, I have seen some serious sucking up, but you may have set a new low," chided another. The men's restroom was roaring.

I have seen this phenomenon occur over and over in business. People in a meeting will nod and agree with everything being said. Heck, they'll even fill out evaluation forms saying the training was "superb," but go into the restroom and say the whole thing was a huge waste of time.

I don't know what really goes on in women's restrooms, but I think most conversations are about women's issues and other heavy-duty topics. I have had fleeting glances at the interior of their rooms, and many of them have couches, big mirrors, nice lighting, etc. Men's rooms are not places you want to hang around for extended periods.

All in all, it never fails. The truth always comes out in the restroom.

CHAPTER
35

Corporate Policies: Real Employee Ego-Boosters

A ny time you think companies are all big, happy families, you should either try to kick your drug habit or admit yourself for therapy. If your family operates the same as the "corporate" family, then you are in deep doo-doo.

It has always amazed me how company policies treat different groups of employees differently. An example was the snow policy that our famed HR people issued.

The policy said basically that if you were a salaried employee, if you made it into work at all when the snow was bad, then you got paid for a full day's work. You could come in for 10 minutes, discuss sporting events, and go home, and receive full pay.

However, if you were an hourly employee and made it into work, then you were paid only for the time you were there. If you came in for 10 minutes, you were paid for 10 minutes.

And, if that didn't bring the caste system home, salaried people could call in and say "I'll be working from home today" and not even attempt to make it in. The secretaries would have to risk their lives to come in; however, their bosses could "work from home," which means stay home and watch "Ellen" and receive full pay.

The same is true for expense accounts. If you are a salaried employee, you can spend huge amounts for lunch and dinner. However, hourly employees are often restricted. Policies currently read: "Salaried employees are authorized unlimited luncheon expenditures when entertaining anyone remotely attached to the company. This can include neighbors, relatives, friends who have driven by the company, people who have heard of the company and, in general, are members of the human race."

The policy for hourly employees says something like, "If you are an hourly employee you are allowed to spend up to $2.00 per lunch (or $4.50 for dinner) if you are with a client of the company in February of even-numbered years. Any expenses that do not fall under these guidelines will not be reimbursed."

What has changed over time is that a salaried employee is expected to work more than 40 hours per week. When you are working 50 or 60 hours a week, your hourly wage can sometimes be below the hourly workers' pay.

CHAPTER

36

Giving Birth To An Elephant: The Evaluation Process

Few things cause as much turmoil in an organization as when annual evaluations are due. The process is like giving birth to an elephant.

Early in my career I thought that the evaluation process was a comprehensive exercise whereby supervisors examined all facets of an employee's work performance and then developed a fair rating.

This was done with great gnashing of teeth and with the highest integrity. This rating then decided your raise and generally your career path.

If you think this is the way it works, then I hate to tell you, the light's on, but nobody's home. Here are some guidelines to tell when your evaluation is not going to go well:

- When your supervisor starts dropping hints that a certain ranking—like a 3 on a 1 (highest) to 5 (lowest) scale is really a "very good" rating. Last year it was considered "average."
- When it is mentioned discreetly that "Boy, the boss didn't like the misspellings in your report on widgets last May."
- When it is mentioned by a supervisor to no one in particular that "Gee, we should all be glad to just have jobs in this economy."

Early on I used to think the process was very objective and honest. Then, I rose up the ladder to the level where I learned differently.

First off, decisions about rankings are often made months ahead of the evaluation process. Most are made when budgets are compiled for the year, which means your raise had been computed without any regard to your performance.

This is a true story. Four of us were called into the boss's office to discuss raises for the people under us. I compiled previous evaluations, how my people had done on their goals for this year, their performance, etc.

"Let's get to it," the boss said in his best command voice. "Let's do Suzy's evaluation." Since Suzy worked for me, I went through her performance step-by-step and came to the grand conclusion that I thought a "2" ranking would be appropriate.

"Geez, John, she's a pain in the ass," said the boss.

"Yes, she can be," I said, "but she is a hard worker and has achieved her objectives."

"John, she's already got more money than God," said another. "Anyway, her husband's a pain in the ass."

Giving Birth To An Elephant: The Evaluation Process

"What the hell difference does it make if her husband blows bubbles out his butt?" I said. "We are ranking her performance, not her wealth, family matters or other personal things."

"John, we have a limited amount of money to give out," noted the boss. "We don't have time to argue over every person. I think that if *you* want a good evaluation, you should show you are a team player.

"Let's take a vote. I say we give Suzy a 3 rating." Everyone nodded in agreement.

The bottom line is, don't try to over-analyze why you were given a particular rating. In most instances, more time is devoted to deciding what to order for lunch in a given day.

CHAPTER

3 7

Some Final Thoughts…

Writing this book went from being a chore to a labor of love. Okay, maybe not "love," but more of a "like."

If I seemed like I was complaining about my life in PR, I apologize. Sure, my nose is a bit brown, but overall, it has been a wonderful career, and I have worked with fascinating folks, from Vice President Cheney and Walter Cronkite to complete lunkheads. If nothing else, they all were interesting.

When you are in PR, sometimes it seems as if you are the one of only a handful of people who knew all along that the Wizard of Oz was really the guy behind the curtain. Much of my job was protecting the Wizard's image.

As an example, one president I worked with wanted to show employees he cared, so he had us buy a machine that signed his name perfectly. It had a template of his actual signature.

He would send out notes all the time that looked like he actually signed them, since the machine used real ink pens. I once had to spend hours having the machine sign those "We love United Way and want your money" letters to employees. It was boring as hell.

Unfortunately, when I am bored, I often do dumb things. A co-worker had recently screwed up something minor, so I wrote a fake note asking for his resignation. Of course, I signed the president's name to it.

I put it on my co-worker's desk. When he returned from lunch and saw the note, he yelled out, "Why, that SOB thinks I am going to resign! I'll let him know what he can do with this $%&^** job!"

Miraculously, I was able to catch him a few steps from actually running into the president's office to ream him out. He would have likely lost his job (and mine in the process).

When I told my friend about the prank, he didn't speak to me for nearly four months. Hey, it seemed like a good idea at the time. Boredom causes you to do strange things.

In this book I have had some fun with many executive foibles I have witnessed over the years, but in all honesty it is important to point out that employees can be a real pain and they can take much of the responsibility for the dysfunction in a company.

We once held an employee meeting to discuss how we can all work together for the betterment of the company. Our president would talk about corporate goals and how "there is no I in team." One employee came to the meeting wearing a T-shirt that proclaimed "All Executives Are A—holes." That was a nice touch.

Another one of my companies had a tradition of giving out turkeys to all employees for Thanksgiving. It was a wonderful gift that costs thousands of dollars each year.

However, some employees complained that some other employees' turkeys were a few ounces more than theirs (try buying hundreds of turkeys exactly 20 lbs.). Others asked if they could

Some Final Thoughts…

get hams instead. Others said they were vegetarians and wanted just the money.

Rarely did any employees actually say "Thank You!" for the turkeys. Our president seemed to only hear employee complaints. It was an easy decision for him just to end the program to stop the complaining—and save $$$$.

The same was true for our Christmas party. One company gave employees huge discounts on our products, but some turned around and sold them at garage sales. Even the company softball tournament was eliminated because a few employees would get drunk and act like idiots.

That's what makes PR so fascinating. You have to deal with some strange individuals at all levels of a company and somehow make sense of this huge, dysfunctional "family."

If you are thinking about a career in PR, jump into it with both feet. While I am a firm believer that working first in the news media will help you understand the media better and also give you some much-needed credibility, just take the plunge.

It has been a wild ride. I wouldn't trade it for anything.

—30—

www.ingramcontent.com/pod-product-compliance
Lightning Source LLC
Chambersburg PA
CBHW071013200526
45171CB00007B/127